Model-Driven and Software Product Line Engineering

Model-Driven and Software Product Line Engineering

Hugo Arboleda
Jean-Claude Royer

First published 2012 in Great Britain and the United States by ISTE Ltd and John Wiley & Sons, Inc.

ISTE Ltd
27-37 St George's Road
London SW19 4EU
UK

www.iste.co.uk

John Wiley & Sons, Inc.
111 River Street
Hoboken, NJ 07030
USA

www.wiley.com

© ISTE Ltd 2012

Library of Congress Cataloging-in-Publication Data

Arboleda, Hugo.
Model-driven and software product line engineering / Hugo Arboleda, Jean-Claude Royer.
pages cm
Includes bibliographical references and index.
 ISBN 978-1-84821-427-9
 1. Software product line engineering. 2. Model-driven software architecture. I. Royer, Jean-Claude. II. Title.
 QA76.76.D47A7323 2012
 005.1--dc23

2012028382

British Library Cataloguing-in-Publication Data
A CIP record for this book is available from the British Library
ISBN: 978-1-84821-427-9

Printed and bound in Great Britain by CPI Group (UK) Ltd., Croydon, Surrey CR0 4YY

Table of Contents

Chapter 1

Introduction

For more than 10 years, two independent approaches in software engineering have been emerging: software product line engineering (SPLE) and model-driven engineering (MDE). Software product line engineering is a software process, which puts emphasis on "re-use" organized through a common software architecture [GOM 04]. This process relies on a domain analysis and scoping activity to characterize the products to be delivered. The realization of a concrete application is based on a production plan, and the configuration of the application of the engineering step. Model-driven engineering emphasizes the creation of models that represent the system under consideration at a high level of abstraction. These models are the base on which to implement the application automatically. These two approaches have in common the following concerns: improving productivity, increasing the quality of software and automating, as much as possible, the construction of software assets. They are also complementary: model-driven engineering seems a promising trend to automate the production chain needed for product creation in product lines. It also seems suited for modeling the various concerns and artifacts of a product line. In software engineering, traceability is the ability to track the information flow of software artifacts. Traceability is also a crucial issue in product line engineering. MDE can help in managing artifacts and tracing links.

The main focus of this book is to propose a practical approach to engineering a software product line based on MDE. This book presents the basic concepts of both engineering approaches and the main challenges in defining a model-driven tool. The book is concerned with the technical aspects of modeling variability, defining a reference architecture, and constructing tool support. This book can be useful for graduate students as well as software engineers who wish to learn about product lines and concepts of model-driven engineering. Two application examples illustrate the concepts and the processes: a product line of Smart-Homes and a product line of Collection Managers. It is also appropriate for researchers in the area of MDE and SPLE since it addresses some complex issues such as fine-grained configuration and fine-grained variation.

1.1. Software product line engineering

Software engineering aims at speeding up software development and maintenance processes, decreasing costs, and improving productivity and quality. By addressing these objectives, software product line engineering seeks to develop software products through the re-use of artifacts. Thus, the products should be quickly developed, and their quality should be as good as the quality of the artifacts used for their construction. A software product line (SPL) is defined as a set of similar products created from re-usable artifacts in the context of a specific application domain. In SPLE, product designers configure and derive products by re-using the available artifacts created by the product line architects. The description of the set of products that are part of an SPL is called the scope of the product line. To capture and express the scope of SPLs, product line architects first determine the commonalities, i.e. the characteristics shared by all products in the scope, and then they study their variability. The architects build a feature model or, more generally, a variability model. This model is a structured set of variation points associated with their *variants*, which can be either requirements, code, architectures, testing plans, or any other elements of a full software development process. Variation points are relevant characteristics that can have different values, the so-called "variants", according to the variability of a product line. The set of re-usable artifacts occurring in the products defines the product line platform. In this book, it shall be referred to as the *core asset*.

The development of the product and core asset are fairly complex processes, often presented with two phases: domain engineering and application engineering. The former process analyzes the domain, the commonalities, and the variability; it elaborates a production plan for the product line development and generates the assets to be re-used. The latter process is in charge of building each product from its characteristics, the core assets and the plan defined during the first phase. This second phase can be a complete software lifecycle: the most important activities are the product configuration and the product derivation. The product configuration is a representation of the product to be built expressed in terms of the variability model. It is from such configuration, core assets, and production plan that the effective product can be generated.

1.2. Model-driven engineering

Model-driven engineering refers to a range of development approaches based on the use of software modeling as primary documents. These documents comprise requirements or other artifacts such as feature models, use cases, Unified Modeling Language (UML) diagrams, and architectures, among others. Code is written by hand or generated in part or in whole from the models. Whenever possible, code generation ranges from system "stubs" or "skeletons" to deployable products. Several steps are required to iteratively integrate various concerns and to transform models until the source code is obtained. Models are less sensitive to computing technology and to evolutionary changes of that technology. We can have general models describing the problem space and deriving other distinct models representing some solutions. Platform-specific aspects, such as the characteristics of languages, can be integrated in subsequent steps and then performance issues or deployment aspects can be further added. In this way, abstraction and separation of concerns can be used in a uniform and tool-assisted process. The need for such facilities is increasing as the semantic gap between modeling languages and implementation codes becomes wider-and-wider.

MDE originated in the late 1990s out of the need for more abstract software description, and to increase software productivity and quality. It emerged from the adoption of UML as a standard and from research on data representation, CASE tools, and interchange format. MDE emphasizes such concerns as abstraction, early verification, model transformation, and automatic code generation. MDE provides a unified formalism with models and transformations to represent artifacts and processes of software engineering. The ability to build readable models is important for stakeholders to collaborate efficiently. Models only capture single points of view and focus on some domain concepts that are known to be easier to specify, understand, and maintain.

Software engineering needs automation. This is a fact learned from the history of engineering. Automation is by far the most effective technological means for boosting productivity and reliability. MDE provides automation at every step of development and facilitates a progressive integration of knowledge and platform details. The techniques and tools for using MDE successfully have now reached a degree of maturity that renders them practical even in large-scale industrial applications.

MDE appears as a promising technique for SPLE since it provides uniformity and abstraction for software artifacts and processes. SPLE is a paradigm that focuses on artifact re-use and variability management. It introduces a complex software process and artifacts that are more numerous, heterogeneous, and complex than in traditional software engineering. MDE can help in representing the artifacts in a uniform and abstract way. SPLE also requires some specific tasks such as product configuration and should place more emphasis on traceability management. MDE has the ability to build complex transformations, which is promising in the automation of domain and application engineering.

1.3. Merging model-driven and software product line engineering

SPLE and MDE have common concerns: improving productivity, making software development cost-effective, empowering domain experts in software development, enforcing architecture, capturing domain and technological knowledge in separate artifacts, increasing software quality, and automating the construction of software products as much as possible. They are also complementary. Model-driven engineering seems a promising trend in automating the production chain needed for the creation of product lines. It is also suited to model the various concerns and artifacts of a product line. SPLE proposes a global view and process for product line engineering with a strong focus on the rational re-use of artifacts.

Many approaches to create SPLs based on MDE have emerged e.g. [VÖL 07b, WAG 05]. These are called *MDE-based SPL approaches* or *MD-SPL* approaches. MDE conceives the whole software development cycle as a process of creation, iterative refinement, and the integration of models. We define an MD-SPL as a set of products developed from application domain models, and derived from a set of re-usable model transformation rules. There is a general agreement on the fact that model transformations may require several stages, e.g. [VÖL 07b, ARB 09b, ARB 09a]. At each stage, application domain models are automatically transformed to include more implementation details. Models with only problem space concerns are incrementally transformed to include the solution space, i.e. concerns of software design and/or technological platforms, as well as performance issues. At the end of a staged model transformation process, models including all the implementation details are transformed into source code of software systems.

Most of the current MD-SPL approaches [VÖL 07b, WAG 05, LOU 08, SAN 08] create application domain metamodels and variability models to capture and express variability *separately*. For configuring a particular product, the product designers create *configurations* that consist of (1) application domain models and (2) *instances* of variability models. An instance of a variability model includes a selection of variants from the variability model. The MD-SPL approaches using multi-staged model transformations also facilitate the configuration of products by creating specific instances of variability models. For example, product designers can select software architectural details before executing model transformations in charge of adding architectural information. Therefore, the staged transformation of an application domain model may derive products with different software architectures or products to run on different technological platforms.

During the product derivation process, the instances of variability models are used to decide what transformation rules must apply. Thus, from different instances of variability models, different products can be derived from the same application domain model.

Figure 1.1 sketches the process of creating an MD-SPL example. Each product line member manages its data by means of a relational database schema. In this example, product line architects have chosen to use the UML Class Metamodel to capture and express the variability related to problem space concerns. Thus, product designers are able to start the configuration process of products by creating diverse class models. To capture variability in the context of relational database schemas, product line architects create a variability model that includes one variation point, a Primary Key Structure with two alternative variants: With Primary Key and Without Primary Key. Additionally, the architects relate a different model transformation rule to each variant. Rule One is related to the variant With Primary Key

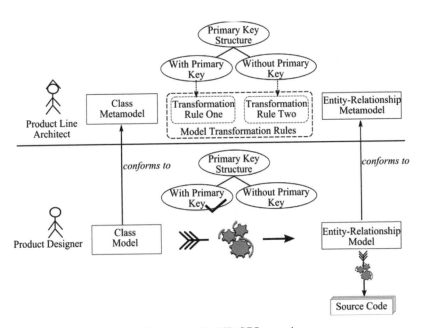

Figure 1.1. *Example of a MD-SPL creation process*

and `Rule Two` is related to the variant `Without Primary Key`. Product designers complete the configuration process of products by creating instances of the variability model. If the variant `With Primary Key` is selected in an instance of the variability model, using `Rule One`, all the class elements in a `Source Class Model` are transformed into table elements with one primary key. If the variant `Without Primary Key` is selected in another instance of the variability model, using `Rule Two`, all the class elements in a `Source Class Model` are transformed into table elements without a primary key.

1.4. The FieSta framework

This book covers most of the creation lifecycle of MD-SPL. The activities have been organized in a framework that incorporates the principles of MD and SPL engineering. We have named this framework FieSta for fine-grained scope definition, configuration, and derivation of model-driven and software product lines. FieSta focuses on two major processes. Firstly, the process of capturing and expressing variability in MD-SPL, which impacts, consequently, on the process of configuring product line members. Secondly, the process of deriving products by re-using and composing model transformations based on product configurations.

FieSta provides model-based mechanisms to extend the expressive power of variability involved in current MD-SPL approaches in such a way that more detailed products can be configured according to the fine-grained variability principle. FieSta includes a mechanism that allows product designers to create *fine-grained configurations* that represent *valid* products. We define a valid product as an assembly that meets the requirements that product designers specify by means of configurations. FieSta also includes a mechanism to control the valid fine-grained variations. FieSta resolves problems in application domains where (1) model elements must be configured individually and (2) products must be configured in multiple stages, sometimes by designers with different domain knowledge.

During the process of product derivation, model transformation rules must be composed to derive products from their configuration. The composition is done according to each configuration. FieSta maintains uncoupled the information of relationships between variants and their related transformation rules. This facilitates the maintenance, re-use, and evolution of transformation rules and/or variability models. Additionally, FieSta proposes a high-level mechanism to compose model transformation rules and to adapt their execution ordering (or execution scheduling) to create fine-grained configurations and derive products based on them.

FieSta (1) provides mechanisms to extend the power of variability of MD-SPL by using metamodeling and feature modeling conjointly, and (2) integrates a product derivation process, which uses the *decision model* and Aspect-Oriented Programming (AOP) facilitating the re-use, adaptation, and composition of model transformation rules. Figure 1.2 presents an activity diagram summarizing the processes involved in FieSta.

During the domain-engineering process, product line architects create model transformations consisting of sets of transformation rules. Each transformation rule is responsible for producing a part of a final product. Model transformation rules implement algorithms to transform application domain models into refined models (or source code) including concerns from a different level of abstraction. Product line architects also create decision models. Decision models are the basis of our mechanism to derive products including variability. They capture the execution ordering of transformation rules to be performed by the model transformation engine to derive configured products. We use AOP to build the scheduling of the transformation rules, i.e. the order in which transformation

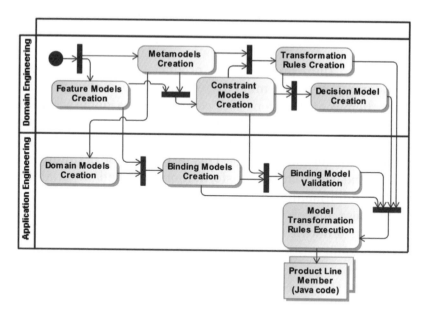

Figure 1.2. *The FieSta general process*

rules are going to process model elements to accomplish the required derivation.

During the domain engineering process, product line architects create application domain metamodels, feature models, and *constraint models* to capture the variability and commonalities of MD-SPL. We introduce constraint models that make it possible for product line architects to capture and express the valid fine-grained variations among product line members using the concepts of *constraint*, *cardinality property*, and *structural dependency property*.

To configure a product during the application engineering process, product designers create (1) application domain models that conform to application domain metamodels and (2) *binding models*, which are sets of bindings between model elements and features. After a binding model is created, it is validated against a set of object constraint language (OCL) statements derived from its respective constraint model.

To derive a complete product according to a binding model, we dynamically adapt the parameters of model transformation executions, which we achieve by using model transformation rules that are selected from the binding model and the pre-created decision models.

Along with FieSta, we present model-based tool support, the FieSta toolkit, which implements facilities to (1) capture fine-grained variations between product line members, (2) configure detailed products, and (3) derive fine-grained configured products. We illustrate the FieSta approach through two application examples: a product line of Smart-Homes and a product line of Collection Managers.

1.5. Book structure

Figure 1.3 presents the structure of this book, which is organized in four parts: an introduction, a presentation of the state-of-the-art, our proposal (the FieSta framework), and the conclusions.

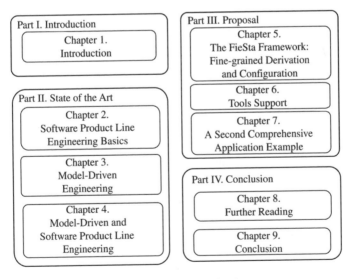

Figure 1.3. *Structure of the document*

Following this chapter, the reader shall find a chapter on software product line engineering, a chapter on model-driven engineering, and a chapter considering the state-of-the-art in model driven and software product line engineering. These chapters provide the foundation for our framework. Part three discusses the FieSta approach. It includes one chapter on the principles of FieSta for fine-grained variation, configuration, and derivation. Following this discussion, we describe the tools for supporting the MD-SPL engineering mechanisms we previously introduced. The concepts and tools are illustrated on a Smart-Home case study. Chapter 7 is devoted to a second application example. The final part is composed of two chapters; the first one presents further readings and the second concludes this book, including a discussion and an outlook for future work.

Chapter 2: Software product line engineering basics. This chapter introduces software product line (SPL) engineering. The major stages in SPL development are discussed: (1) the domain engineering process and (2) the application engineering process. Feature modeling is introduced as a mechanism for expressing product line variability and for configuring products. Decision models are included as artifacts used to relate re-usable core assets and variants from product lines, and support the product derivation process based on product configurations.

Chapter 3: Using model-driven engineering. This chapter introduces the main concepts of MDE: models, metamodels, and model transformations. Regarding models, we introduce some definitions and we explain the concept of *separation of concerns* of a system in different models. We also discuss the concept of *level of abstraction* of models, and we classify the levels of abstraction as a particular case of separation of concerns. We explain the general concepts of metamodeling: domain specific modeling (DSM), the relation of conformity, and the four-layer metamodeling framework. We summarize

UML and OCL notations to help readers understand the models presented in this book. We also introduce the eclipse modeling framework (EMF), which is a metamodeling and modeling framework. Finally, we define the concept of model transformations and we classify them into four major categories: model-to-model, model-to-text, horizontal, and vertical transformations. We introduce the Xpand and the Xtend model transformation languages, which are languages included in the OAW framework.

Chapter 4: Model-driven and software product line engineering. We give an overall view of the process, the challenges of merging these two engineering approaches, and the impact in the problem and solution dimensions. We discuss in depth the variability expression, the multi-stage process, the core asset development, the product configuration, and the product derivation process.

Chapter 5: The FieSta framework. The previous chapters present the background for this chapter in which FieSta, our approach to create SPL based on MDE, is introduced. This chapter makes use of the application example introduced throughout the previous chapters to illustrate the different axes of our framework. Constraint models, which are re-usable artifacts we build to capture the scope of MD-SPLs, are presented and their use is illustrated within the context of the Smart-Home example. Binding models, which serve to configure products and are sets of bindings between model elements and features that satisfy the constraint models, are explained and also illustrated with our application example. We then show how to derive products based on the binding models and the decision models, which are sets of aspects we use to adapt model transformations required to derive configured products. Finally, we present the limitations of FieSta for deriving products based on decision models.

Chapter 6: Tools support. This chapter validates FieSta, our MD-SPL approach, by presenting examples of products that we are able to derive using our MD-SPL mechanisms. It presents the results of configuring and deriving products of the Smart-Home product line. The implementation strategy of FieSta is sketched. It defines the general process for the implementation of our MD-SPL engineering mechanisms for creating product lines. The implementation strategy includes (1) the required activities for the creation of products, and (2) the tools we create to support these activities. The tool support for expressing variability and configuring products, as well as the tool support for deriving configured products are described.

Chapter 7: A Second comprehensive application example. In addition to our Smart-Home systems' MD-SPL, we have also created a product line of stand-alone applications to manage data collections. We call a member of this product line a *collection manager system*. For example, a collection manager system manages the students of a school and their personal information: name, address, e-mail, etc. Another product manages records in a music store and their related information: name, artist, price, etc. At the architecture level, products are structured in two tiers: the kernel and the Graphical User Interface (GUI). The kernel tier implements functional requirements to add elements into the collection and to order the collection. The GUI tier implements visualization and interaction with the final users and the kernel component.

Chapter 8: Further reading. The purpose of this chapter is to provide the main references related to product line engineering and to discuss some open or more advanced issues. This chapter reviews some of the previous books related to product lines and to model-driven approaches. For historical and pedagogical reasons, we comment on Northrop's and Pohl's books. Gomaa's book promotes a rather UML-like approach for SPLE, while the book is aligned with new technologies such as MDE and AOP. The book from van der Linden *et al.* addresses a survey of product line practices as well as various application examples, being a valuable reference for practitioners who want to launch a product line. A section of this chapter is dedicated to featuring modeling notations, which are of prime importance in SPLE. The problem of mixing product line engineering and model-driven engineering has been already addressed in several works. A specific section is devoted to these approaches, a detailed discussion, and a comparison table are presented. An advanced topic, not yet discussed in the current book, is the management of dynamic information in such an engineering process. Domain Specific Languages (DSL) are nowadays, techniques which are completely relevant in our context. We present some facts concerning the relations between DSL and model-driven engineering. A final section collects several important references to provide readers with a more comprehensive view of this domain.

Chapter 9: Conclusion. This chapter concludes this book presenting (1) a summary of our framework, (2) a reflection taking into account the contributions we propose to the field of model-driven software product line engineering, and (3) future outlooks for research.

Chapter 2

Software Product Line Engineering Basics

Software product line engineering is a recent trend in software development. It can bring benefits in terms of costs and productivity; however, it also involves a complex software development process. This chapter introduces the basics for product line engineering and addresses the main technical aspects. The management of product line engineering processes is an important issue; however, it is not dealt within this book. Interested readers can refer to [NOR 02, POH 05a, CAC 06].

2.1. Introduction to product line engineering

Software systems are complex and their development is time-consuming and error-prone. Many software companies are building applications that share more commonalities than differences. They often repeatedly add new features and build new variants or releases of their applications. Most often, software development consists of creating variations from existing software. The strategy of re-using software artifacts has been seen as a means to alleviate the problems associated with software development. Re-using software artifacts facilitates the composition of products from a set of artifacts already developed and tested, instead of building the products from scratch. Software product line engineering is a paradigm that provides a means to incorporate the re-use strategy as a central part of software development [CLE 01, BOS 02]. A software product line (SPL) is a set of software products that share many common properties to be built from a common set of assets [CZA 00]. The ultimate objective of product line engineering is to improve productivity, i.e. save time, reduce costs, and increase the quality of products. In this chapter, we first introduce the basis of SPL engineering (SPLE), including the main processes involved in the creation of SPLs: *domain engineering process*, section 2.5, and *application engineering process*, section 2.7. These two processes are also often called "development for re-use" and "development with re-use", placing strong emphasis on re-usability.

The principle of SPLE is to develop several products sharing some common concerns in a development cycle.

DEFINITION 2.1. – *A software product line is a set of software applications that shares concerns, features, requirements, or market specificity and that are built in a rational and planned way from a set of re-usable assets.*

Mainly used in Europe, the term *product family* can be considered as a synonym. The term *software factory* is a related and older concept, but it is not equivalent and covers various meanings. It was used earlier to denote product lines and it is still used, specifically in the Microsoft context. Often, a software factory denotes a new generation framework trying to automate the application engineering as much as possible. This concept emerges from model-driven engineering and some new generative approaches making the definition of complex and automated tool chains possible. A software factory can be a part of an SPL, namely in the latest generation where application engineering is strongly automated. However, product line is a broader concept that includes variability management and domain analysis, which are not considered in a software factory.

The first thing to note about SPLE is that the development cycle produces several products or applications, while most of the traditional development cycles focus on one application at a time. The second point is that the products share some concerns; usually, one can say that they belong to the same domain. For instance, we can have several configurations for Smart-Home that are more or less secure, autonomous, interconnected with the Web and so on. The common parts define what is called the *commonalities*. All Smart-Homes should have at least rooms, doors, windows, and a heating system. However, these products are different, thus, they have some specific parts. The set of these differences is called *the variability*. For instance, we can define a basic home with a security system, another one with automatic windows, and a third one with both features. One important task in SPLE is to define precisely the domain of interest, to express the commonalities and the variability of the products, and to structure this information.

A simple and abstract view of the main processes involved in SPLE is depicted in Figure 2.1. It involves three interacting and iterative processes. The *management* process is under the control of the business plan which decides the production of applications. It acts as a supervisor for the two other processes. It looks at the quality of the core assets and the final products. The *core assets development* is responsible for developing individual elements (e.g. requirements, codes, tests, documentations) and to make them re-usable. It also defines the product line scope and elaborates a production plan. The former describes the set of products while the latter shows how to build the products. The *products development* is responsible for the building of products following the production plan. It starts from a configuration of the product, which is a description of its included features, and it then builds the expected product application using the core assets but also suggesting new assets if needed. These three processes are orchestrated by the management process but they are all strongly interacting.

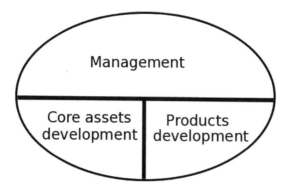

Figure 2.1. *The three processes view*

Here, we concentrate on technical engineering activities rather than on project management. Effective technical engineering is presented in two phases: *domain engineering* and *application engineering*. The first engineering step analyzes the domain, the commonalities, and the variability. It elaborates a global and common production plan and generates the assets to be re-used. The second engineering step is responsible for building one product from its characteristics, the core assets, and the plan defined during the first step. The plan can be an informal document describing how to build the products. The future trend in SPLE is to automate the production plan, and one successful technique is to use MDE to define an executable tool chain. These steps will be described in more detail in the rest of the book. Another point to bear in mind is the difference between the problem space and the solution space traditionally used in software engineering. The problem space is the set of requirements, the need for some applications, regardless of the precise structure and shape of this information. Its goal is to describe the functionality of the system, but often non-functional requirements are also added, such as performance or even marketing requirements. The solution space is concerned with the description of one solution to the problem using various notations ranging from message sequences, architecture, class diagrams, or source codes. The interplay between the two engineering steps, problem and solution space, and core assets is depicted in Figure 2.2. In this picture, we simplify the development process during engineering when all the steps of a classic lifecycle are relevant. Thus, we should add tests, maintenance, documentation, versioning, etc.

In this diagram, the core assets form a central repository to store and mine assets. These assets can be produced by all the steps; they are referenced in the production plan and effectively used in application engineering to build products.

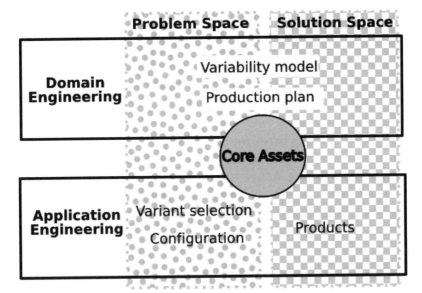

Figure 2.2. *Domain and application engineering*

2.2. Brief history

The notion of the product line is rather old; Wikipedia argues that the oldest assembly line is "The Terracotta Army" around the year 215 BC before Christian era. (http://en. wikipedia.org/wiki/Assembly_line#Overview:_a_culmination _of_many_efforts). The most famous and more recent assembly line was introduced by the car manufacturer H. Ford around 1913 as the result of the efforts of several engineers over seven years. The assembly line decreased car production costs mainly by reducing the assembly time. It paved the way for mass production but also influenced the industry considerably. The history of software product lines started 30 years ago. There are some differences between classic manufactured products and software systems. For instance, making an exact copy of a type of software is easy and there are often many possible variations. Software engineering is not the straight application of industry engineering to software. This engineering is still exploring new approaches and product lines are a normal evolution of software engineering. The advent of SPLE is comparatively recent and the first Software Product Line Conference, organized by the Software Engineering Institute, was held in 2000. [SUG 06] introduces a special issue of CACM dedicated to software product lines.

This history has three foundations: Artifact re-use, program families, and domain analysis. The paper from Mc Ilroy [McI 68] is the main source for re-usability and software component concepts. The idea was to build software applications like hardware systems, by assembling pre-defined components. Parnas [PAR 76] introduced the notion of program families in the middle of the 1970s. It can be viewed as a forerunner of the software product family concept but dealing only with the design step. The notion of domain analysis was introduced in the middle of the 1980s by Neighbors [NEI 89]. He introduced the Draco approach to the construction of software systems from re-usable components. *"The basic idea captures the frustrating feeling that most of the system you are currently building is the same as the last few systems you have built; but once again you are building everything from scratch"*. This work exposes the three major stakeholders in domain analysis: the application domain analyst, the modeling domain analyst, and the domain designer.

The first industrial project was the Toshiba Software Factory in 1977; it concerns the development of a family of power generators. One useful reference about the activity in this domain is the SEI site (http://www.sei.cmu.edu/productlines/), which contains information about case studies, tools, and methods as well as a catalog of software product line projects. Northrop, in [NOR 02], was the first author to propose a comprehensive view of SPLE with all the related technical and organizational activities. The SEI group was also at the origin of the patterns for categorizing SPL practices. At the beginning of 1980s, the European community sponsored several important projects in this domain such as ESAPS, CAFE, FAMILIES and more recently AMPLE (www.ample-projet.net). Another sign of the activity in this domain was the launching of conferences: the two main ones are Software Product Line and Product Family Engineering conferences that were merged in 2005. More details on these past events can be found on the SPLC website (http://www.splc.net/history.html).

The SPL success story of product line engineering includes HP printers, Nokia smart phones, and many others. HP developed a line of firmware for a number of printers and multifunction (printer/copier/scanner/fax) devices. These products have been created with a quarter of the team, in a third of the time, and with 1/25th the number of bugs in earlier products. Nokia Mobile Phones produces a wide range of mobile phones, more than 30 models, with a wide variety of functional features, different user interfaces, and using several platforms. Nokia is a leader in mobile phone manufacture, and software product line engineering has helped them reach that position. MARKET MAKER provides software in Europe for the stock market. The company decided to plan the Internet versions as a software product line. Due to its systematic product line approach, the company was able to set up products in a few days. The time to market is 2-4 days and after five products, there is a reduction of 60% in maintenance costs. More details can be found in the hall of fame (http://www.splc.net/fame.html) on the SPLC website.

2.3. Application example: Smart-Home systems

To better explain the basis of MDE and SPLE, and to demonstrate the feasibility and economies of our approach, we consider two examples from two different domains. In this chapter, we introduce the first one. This is a home automation system, which is rather a classic application of product lines. The second one is introduced and developed in Chapter 7. It has more characteristics of information system applications where we need to manage, present, and store several pieces of information of a business domain.

The Smart-Home illustrative example is taken from the domain of home automation. *"A smart home is a building for living equipped with a set of electrical and electronic sensors and actuators in order to allow for an intelligent sensing and controlling of the building's devices: windows, heaters, lights, etc."* [ELS 08]. This application example was also exploited in several other projects, for instance in the AMPLE project [RAS 11] and in Pohl's book [POH 05b].

2.3.1. *Smart-Home system's domain*

Smart-Homes are equipped with a wide range of electronic and electrical devices, such as light arrays, temperature sensors, thermostats, electrically steered blinds and windows, door sensors, door openers, etc. A Smart-Home software system coordinates and controls such devices enabling inhabitants to manage them from a common user interface. A Smart-Home system offers high-level functionality where several sensors and actuators work together. The sensors are physical devices that measure values of the environment and make them available to the Smart-Home system. The actuators activate the devices whose state can be monitored and changed. All installed devices, including sensors and actuators, are a part of the Smart-Home network. The status of devices can be changed by inhabitants through the user interface, remotely by using an Internet connection or by the system using predefined policies. These policies let the system act autonomously in case of certain events. For example, in case of low indoor temperature, the windows close automatically; in case of fire, the fire brigade is automatically called, and so on.

The architectural structure of buildings (e.g. the number of floors, rooms, or windows), the sensors and actuators as well as other devices, their location inside the buildings, and the policies, are specific for each Smart-Home system and must be defined by the designers of the Smart-Home systems. Thus, Smart-Home systems can be created with the necessary software components to respond to the particular requirements of each Smart-Home owner. At runtime, the Smart-Home system is then ready to respond to external or internal stimuli depending on the defined structure of the building, its devices, and the chosen policies.

In our example, Smart-Home systems must provide the following functions:

– *Climate control system.* Climate control devices must be orchestrated to keep the preferred temperature in the rooms of the house.

– *Security system.* The door, the window sensors, and the motion detectors should detect unauthorized entries into the house. If any attempt at intrusion is detected, emergency action must be taken.

– *Energy saving.* House devices should be orchestrated to use the least amount of energy.

The objective of this application example is to generate software applications that simulate the interactions and behaviors of home automation systems.

2.3.2. Requirements of the application example

Several types of houses, different customer demands, the need for short time-to-market, and cost saving are the main causes for variability and create a demand for product lines of Smart-Home systems. We characterize the product line of a Smart-Home system according to the following three sources of variability:

– *House architectural structure.* Each house has its particular architectural structure with several floors, rooms, stairs, doors, and windows.

– *Smart-Home facilities.* Each house is equipped with several facilities related to controlled devices.

– *Software architecture.* Each Smart-Home system has a technology platform integrating its devices under different software architectures.

The objective of this application example is to develop diverse Smart-Home systems which (1) are able to manage particular variants of Smart-Homes and (2) only include the necessary software components to satisfy the requirements of Smart-Home's owners. It is not our aim to develop only one Smart-Home system, which can be dynamically configured to support the considered variability. The following subsections describe in more detail the particular variants related to each of the three sources of variability considered in our product line.

2.3.2.1. *House architectural structure*

The structure of houses is the most evident source of variation. The description of a house includes structural elements such as floors and rooms. In our application example, we take into account the following structural elements: floors, rooms, staircases, doors, and windows. Thus, houses can have different number of floors; floors can have different number of rooms; rooms can have different number of windows or doors; staircases connect the different floors in the house, and so on. Therefore, the configuration of the architectural structure of houses must be performed by *building architects*.

2.3.2.2. Smart-Home's facilities

We take into account the need for incorporating automation facilities for houses that are independent to the house structure. By orthogonal, we mean facilities that affect multiple structural entities. These facilities allow autonomous actions according to the defined policies. Houses include electrical and electronic devices such as automatic lights, electric windows, security devices as alarms, and security systems for authentication. These devices, and therefore their actuation, are related to optional facilities that the designer has to select and bind to other elements that already exist in the house. For instance, the automatic lights can be bound to all rooms in the house or the security alarm system can be bound only to the main entrance door.

For this application example, we consider two groups of facilities. The first group is related to access control facilities. The second one is related to environmental control facilities:

– *Access control*. This facility group should insure that only inhabitants and authorized visitors can enter into the house. Two alternative options must be provided to control the access of inhabitants: (1) keypad authentication and (2) fingerprint authentication.

– *Environmental control*. This facility adds the capability of measuring the indoor temperature and takes some action according to pre-defined policies. Two alternative options must be provided for environmental control: (1) automatic windows and (2) air-conditioning. Automatic windows must be automatically opened if the temperature in a room rises above a certain threshold and closed if the temperature falls under a certain threshold. Similarly, air conditioning is turned on if the temperature in a room rises above a certain threshold and turned off if the temperature falls under a certain point.

The configuration of Smart-Homes facilities is in the charge of domain experts who know how to set up houses including devices such as sensors and actuators. *Facilities designers* must also support owners of houses to take decisions about the distribution of devices, for example to save costs of construction and maintenance of Smart-Home systems.

2.3.2.3. *Software architecture*

We build Smart-Home systems using a component-based development strategy. We create components to manage the different devices included in Smart-Home systems. For our application example, we use OSGi (Open Services Gateway Initiative) [OSG 09] as our base component integration platform because it is currently the preferred platform for home automation. See also [RAS 11].

We classify software components according to their type (*active* or *passive* components) and their instantiation mode (*Deployment* or *Invocation*). Thus, the architecture of Smart-Home systems can vary depending on the type of components we create to manage the devices and their instantiation mode:

−*Active and passive components*. Active components are components offering one service periodically. The infrastructure invokes this service periodically after a configurable time period. Active components have their own threads of control and they are started once the component is activated. Passive components offer on-demand services to other components. The type of a component depends on the services provided by the component. For instance, a component providing a service to open/close automatic windows according to the temperature of rooms is an active component. This component could check the temperature of rooms periodically to open/close the automatic windows. A component providing services to open/close doors only when inhabitants arrive is a better candidate to be a passive one.

− *Instantiation mode: on deployment or on invocation.* A component can be instantiated either when it is deployed or when one of its services is invoked (lazy deployment).

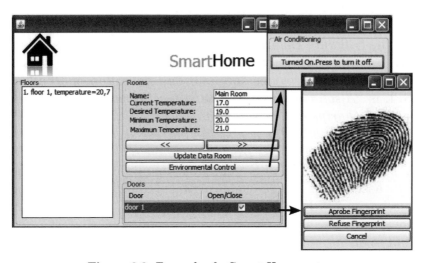

Figure 2.3. *Example of a Smart-Home system*

The configuration of the software architecture of Smart-Home systems is driven by software architects who are experienced in taking software design decisions. Each different source of variability is the responsibility of a particular expert that has the skills required to configure this aspect of Smart-Home systems. In our application example, these are the *building architect*, the *facilities designer*, and the *software architect*. This is the main reason that implies the use of a staged-configuration mechanism. The configuration process is, thus, a combination of several stages dedicated to a variability aspect and a particular expert of this bearing.

Figure 2.3 is an example of the GUI (graphical user interfaces) corresponding to one Smart-Home System. This

Smart-Home system has one floor with two rooms, the Main Room and the Living Room. Figure 2.3 presents the Main Room, which has Air Conditioning as the Environmental Control, and its door has Fingerprint as the Door Lock Control.

2.4. Software product line engineering

The Software Engineering Institute (SEI) [CAR 09], which has been the most important promoter of the software product line paradigm, provides the following definition of what an SPL is: *"A software product line is a set of software-intensive systems sharing a common, managed set of features that satisfy the specific needs of a particular market segment or mission and that are developed from a common set of core assets in a prescribed way"* [CLE 01]. This definition uses the term core asset, which are re-usable artifacts considered as building blocks in SPLE. These re-usable artifacts can be models, common components, documentation, requirements, test cases, and so on.

To obtain benefits from the creation of re-usable common assets, it is important to be able to derive many products from the assets. In SPLE, the description of the set of products, which are parts of an SPL, is called the *scope of the product line*. To achieve a profitable SPL, its scope must be neither very large nor very small. To capture the scope of SPLs, product line architects determine the commonalities, i.e. the characteristics shared by all products in a product line, and the ways in which they can vary (variability). If the ratio between the commonality and the variability is low, then the core assets will lose their ability to satisfy the variability; economy of product derivation will be lost, and the product line will fall into the traditional style of "one-product-per-time". If the scope is very small, then the core assets might not be built in a generic enough way, and the return on investment will never be achieved [CLE 02a, CLE 01]. The management of variability is the most important activity in SPL development. It is a transverse activity performed during the whole product line development cycle.

Figure 2.4 summarizes the five main activities involved in the two SPL engineering processes. In this figure, variability management covers the entire domain engineering since several kinds of variability and several stages are needed. The core assets result from domain engineering; this is "for re-use", while product derivation re-uses the elements from the core assets. The product configuration can be seen as creating a specific instance of the variability model built during domain engineering. The production plan is the main activity responsible for the derivation of each product. The following sections detail these activities.

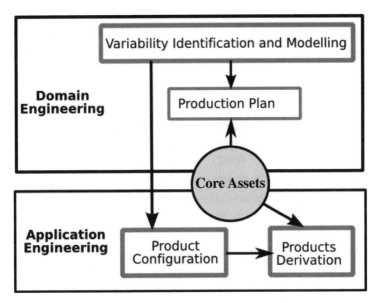

Figure 2.4. *The processes of domain and application engineering*

Several dimensions are interesting for SPLE: the adoption of SPLE, the development process, the re-use organization, and the technical aspects.

The adoption of SPLE by a company is an important problem, for which, not much research has been undertaken. However, [CLE 02b, CLE 06] present some results on this subject. Adoption requires an initial investment and the coordination of several business and technical activities. In [CLE 06] the authors argue the need for re-using an "Adoption Factory" to coordinate these practices for successfully initiating a product line. As explained by Krueger in [KRU 06] the first generation of SPL methods rely on manual techniques to build products. The next generation of methods offers another step forward with bounded variability combinations and software mass customization. This new generation will minimize the adoption barrier by automating application engineering and reducing the number of product configurations. In this book, we will focus on the process and technical aspects related to MDE. The techniques presented here, like the automated application engineering with configurators and the creation of feature model configurations, are completely aligned with this new generation.

To run an SPLE process, three main ways have been identified in the literature: proactive, reactive, or extractive (see [FRA 05, CLE 02b]). In the *proactive* process, the engineering starts from scratch, analyzes the domain, builds the reference architecture, the core assets, and then generates the products. There is an important investment at the beginning to start the line and precise management must be done to evaluate the benefits. It will be successful in a mature and stable domain where it is possible to know in advance the features and the product characteristics. The *reactive* process is a way to dynamically develop and extend the product line. It starts with an existing product line or a product and then builds the variability models with new products and new features. This is suitable for a domain where products are not stable or not known when the product line begins. It does not need a significant initial investment but the re-factoring of assets during the product line evolution is complex. Evolution in software engineering is an intricate problem and it is increasing with SPLE. The latest method is called *extractive*: It starts with a family of existing products, which will be transformed in a product line. Thus, the company has a good knowledge of the domain and the applications to build. This is an interesting way for companies having some application domains and wanting to quickly adopt SPLE. In this book, we will focus on proactive product lines; however, most of the techniques used apply to the other approaches.

Another process characterization was illustrated in [RAS 11]; it is related to the kind of products the company has to build with regard to its business model. In the *product-oriented* approach the products are well identified and are expected to be sold a number of times. The number of different products is stable and they are mastered by the company. However, new features can be added to some products in the line, thus, facilitating product line evolution. Multimedia systems or mobile phone applications are examples for which we can expect to automate the product generation as much as possible. Hence, the focus is on maintenance and evolution of the product lines to get benefits. The *solution-oriented* is quite adequate to manage a set of products for which the variability analysis is difficult; for instance, if the products are too numerous. It is the case that if products are sold only once; each product is different from the previous one, but they share some commonalities. It is rather difficult to automate the product derivation, but it is convenient to use SPLE to get a more rational process than a simple copy-and-paste paradigm. For instance, web applications for enterprises are often very similar but different in many details about their content, interactions, and presentations. In this approach, the degree of automation provided by the software factory is considered more crucial than scoping the domain. These orientations and ways are not completely orthogonal. For instance, the solution-oriented approach can be viewed as the initial step of any reactive product line engineering. That is, once the solution-oriented approach has been completed, the reactive team could lift up specific product analysis/design/coding done in application engineering and improve domain engineering to evolve the product line.

The organization of the re-use is an important factor for the benefits of a product line. However, it requires an initial investment and it pays off only after the assets are re-used in several products. It seems that in any case, a good management of the re-use needs centralization. A completely distributed management of the core assets is risky; the focus of the product line may diverge. The critical technical aspects are numerous and many different points have to be considered for the success of an SPLE process. Some of these are discussed in this book and in further detail in this section. An important one is variability management, but also the building of the architecture reference, and the chain for product derivation. Testing, evolution, traceability, and quality management are of great importance; they are usual in the traditional software development process but in SPLE they have new characteristics and they are more complex. Some of these issues are briefly discussed in section 2.9.

2.5. Domain engineering

Domain engineering is the process of SPL engineering in which the commonality and the variability of the product line are defined [POH 05b]. The development of an SPL starts with the analysis and modeling of common and variable features of the product line. A domain analysis, which limits the product line scope, is performed. In a second step, commonality and variability are identified, classified, and documented. During this engineering, re-usable core assets are built to fulfill the identified and classified variations. Finally, a production plan is defined, which is the set of rules to build the products of the domain.

DEFINITION 2.2. – *The product line scope is the set of products that is built by the product line. It defines the business domain, which is the focus of the product line.*

There is no standard way to define this set; an enumeration complemented with informal textual descriptions can be used. The variability management tries to give a more formal description using, for example, feature models and product configurations.

DEFINITION 2.3. – *The core assets are the set of re-usable artifacts that are built and maintained along the product line activities. These assets are the building blocks for the products of the product line.*

The notion of asset or artifact is neutral and can be anything needed in the product line development. That means the usual elements used in software engineering such as requirements, UML, programs in any language, configuration scripts, architectures, documentations, or tests. It can also include performance models, budget estimations, marketing requirements, and so on.

DEFINITION 2.4. – *The production plan is a guide to build the products from the product configuration by re-using and configuring the assets.*

The production plan collects a set of rules to build the products from the configuration, thus, managing the commonality, the variability, and re-using of the assets. The production plan usually defines a reference architecture, which is a way to map all the products to build in a common framework. In the new approach of SPLE based on MDE, this production plan materializes by a chain of transformations. This is then more formal and also paves the way for automatic product derivation.

DEFINITION 2.5. – *The reference architecture is a specification capturing some global properties of the functions, qualities, organizations, and interactions of the products in the product line.*

Its role is to collect, in one single artifact, the overall common and variable knowledge related to the functionality of the products. It can also express the structural organization, qualities, and the connections between the different components of the products. It is architecture, and as such, can be specified in various ways ranging from formal architectural languages to light weight notations and natural languages. One of the main notations is UML with additional stereotypes or constructions such as the UML merging operator. MDE in this context is also used and several metamodels exist [GOM 04, RAS 11]. The reference architecture should represent the product line scope; validation or evaluation has to be performed to ensure this representation. Another aspect is that, like all other re-usable artifacts, the reference architecture can be subject to evolution.

2.5.1. *Component-based software engineering*

One important idea to improve re-usability, which dates back to the McIlroy paper [McI 68], is software components. One can say that component-based software engineering (CBSE) is the root of domain engineering. This principle is extensively exploited in software product lines to define applications by assembling assets. This is suitable in all the development steps where new assets are preferably built from existing assets, and this is also true for final products. To take into account variability, new assets and new links can be added, removed, or changed in a given configuration. Various models of components and composition are of interest; for instance, template, module, software component, architectural description language [MED 00], model and weaving [JÉZ 08], or aspect oriented programming [KIC 97]. As an example, one of the first experiments of software product lines was done by Philips in the mid-1990s. Philips was developing a large range of televisions worldwide. While the hardware was modular, the software parts were developed through a classic approach using mainly compiler switches, runtime options, and code duplication with changes. However, the new products needed more and more functionalities and combinations of these functionalities. The company had to integrate different pieces of software coming from different areas and developed at different times. The existing component technology available at this time was not suited to the existing constraints; thus, Philips designed the Koala component language [OMM 00]. It was inspired by the Darwin language [MAG 96] dedicated to distributed system architectures. Component languages are really akin to implementing software product lines. However, it can raise some unexpected issues as demonstrated in [PAV 04] with the implementation in ArchJava. In this case, the communication integrity property makes the dynamic configuration of composite components difficult. Nevertheless, some solutions exist; for instance, the use of component generators.

2.6. Variability management

Variability management in SPL engineering is the set of activities related to the identification, expression, and binding of common and variable features included in the scope of the product line. The management of variability is of primary importance for product line development. The effectiveness of a product line approach depends on how well it manages the variability throughout the development lifecycle, from early analysis to the final derivation of products [STA 06]. The management of variability in SPLs is the most general and important topic, and it is at the core of the approach we present in Chapter 5. Different definitions related to variability management can be found in the literature. Here, we list two of them, which refer to *variability* and *variability management*.

DEFINITION 2.6. – *The variability of a set of software systems or products is the set of differences, described in a structured way, of some or all of their characteristics.*

There are many methods for classifying and documenting variability in software product lines [CHE 09]. Several approaches for classifying and documenting variability focus on the use of variability models [SIN 07, BAY 06].

From an abstract point of view, variability management can be seen as the definition of *variation points* and *variants*. A variation point is a location point in an artifact where several variants are possible. A variant is a concrete realization of a variation point; it corresponds to an alternative to bind the variation point. There are some characteristics or constraints related to the possible variants, which are attached to the variation point. In a secure Smart-Home, we have authentication requirements (the variation point), which could be more or less sophisticated. The variants are a simple key lock, an electronic keyboard, and various kinds of recognizer devices (e.g. visual, vocal, digital). In the physical architecture of the Smart-Home, we should allow various structures. Thus, we can have one or more floors, each of them with different structures in terms of rooms, doors, windows, etc. Another way to describe this variability is to enumerate a set of predefined alternatives such as standard flat, house, hotel, castle, etc. The Smart-Home structure is a variation point with many complex variants.

DEFINITION 2.7. – *Variability management is the process of making the variability of software artifacts explicit and to enable variant binding throughout the lifecycle.*

Pohl *et al.* [POH 05b] define variability management as the set of activities for defining and exploiting variability throughout the SPL development lifecycle. The concept covers the following issues: (1) supporting activities concerned with variability and commonality analysis, which includes identification and documentation of variability, and (2) supporting activities concerned with variability binding and variability realization, which includes configuration of product line members and derivation of these products. Typically, (1) the variability and commonality analysis is performed during the *domain engineering process*; (2) the variability binding and variability realization is performed during the *application engineering process*.

A distinction is often made between *positive variability* and *negative variability*. In negative variability, the reference architecture builds a product with all the features and a mechanism is responsible to mask or remove non-selected variants. This is a practical response, which is simple but not really scalable. Mechanisms such as C macros (#define and #ifdef) can be used for that. Positive variability is a much more complex mechanism, which builds the product, in a constructive way, with only the selected features. Most of the existing mechanisms allow positive variability. Variability is possible at any level of the software development process and a convenient classification is *essential variability* and *technical variability* introduced by [POH 05b]. While essential variability is related to the requirement of the client, technical variability is that which occurs in the process of realizing it. In the Smart-Home described earlier, the two first variabilities, home architecture and smart-home facilities, are essential variabilities, while software infrastructure is only a technical variability. Since artifacts, products and even the product line are evolving, we must consider *variation in time*, which is the evolution and versions of artifacts along the time. Two products may differ since they have different implementations of the same features; this is *variation in space*.

The variability mechanisms can be classified according to the software development steps or the main concepts they address. A more comprehensive taxonomy of variability realization techniques is described in [SVA 05]. For requirements, we can use the use case notation from UML with specialization, which extends and includes relationships. But the most common is *feature modeling*; however, many approaches are now based on the use of one or several metamodels addressing specific variability concerns. The next subsection explains what feature modeling is; Chapter 3 – MDE will describe the metamodel approach and Chapter 4 will show how to use both ways consistently. At the architecture level, UML construction such as inheritance, the merge operator, and metamodels are of great importance for variability. Due to the deficiency or the non-suitability of existing languages, there are some specific proposals such as the VML4Arch of the AMPLE project [RAS 11][1]. At implementation, there are various ways to express variability in code, ranging from macros (like #define), inheritance, parameterization (template, generic), aspects, feature-oriented programming, and patterns or frameworks. During testing, composition, configuration, and parameterization are classical means to build new test sets. The reader should note that these are rapidly evolving and there will be a variability language in the near future. There is currently an attempt to propose an OMG standard, which is called Common Variability Language (CVL)[2].

2.6.1. *Feature modeling*

The features describe the common and variable functionality of a system under development. The feature modeling notation facilitates the construction of a hierarchical decomposition of features into a tree structure, which represents variation points and variants. As said before, a variation point is a relevant characteristic of a system; for example, the operating system under which a system can run. A variation point can have different values or variants according to the variability of a product line. The features are

---

1 In fact, this book proposes a variability modeling family called VML*.
2 See http://www.omgwiki.org/variability/doku.php for more information.

used to define a specific domain in terms of their *mandatory*, *optional*, or *alternative* characteristics. The commonalities are represented as a tree of mandatory features. Optional denotes characteristics specific to some products and alternatives express a choice between several variants.

Extensions have been introduced to increase the expressive power, such as feature cardinality, groups and group cardinality, and attributes for features. The purpose of these extensions is to restrict the set of variants that can be selected from feature models to create particular configurations. One of the most cited works on feature modeling was done by Czarnecki *et al.* [CZA 04], where the authors propose a *cardinality-based* notation for feature modeling including *solitary*, *group*, and *grouped* features. This approach integrates a number of existing extensions of previous approaches; thus, we suggest the use of this notation.

Figure 2.5 presents a feature model including alternative Smart-Homes' facilities. One FeatureGroup appears for each group of facilities. The Lock Door Control feature groups the features Fingerprint and Keypad and has cardinality [0..1], which *implicitly* means that Door elements can have either keypad, fingerprint, or none of them as lock door control mechanisms. The Environmental Control feature groups the features Air Conditioning and Automatic Windows and also has cardinality [0..1], which *implicitly* means that Room elements can have either automatic windows, air conditioning, or none of them as lock environmental control mechanism. We say *implicitly* because there is no semantics in traditional feature models or in metamodels, to formally denote that features represent variants that affect particular model elements.

Figure 2.6 presents another example to illustrate the concepts introduced by Czarnecki *et al.* by using a feature model of an operating system security profile [CZA 04].

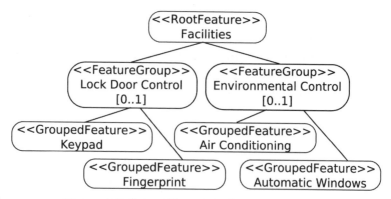

Figure 2.5. *Smart-Homes' facilities feature model*

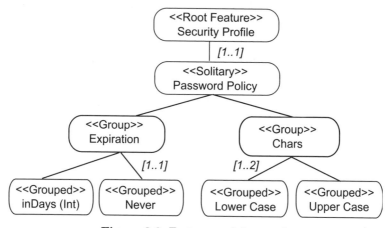

Figure 2.6. *Feature model example*

The `Password Policy` of the `Security Profile` has associated a policy to manage the password `Expiration` date. For the `Password Policy` a `solitary` feature has been created. In this case, the `solitary` feature has associated the cardinality [1..1], which means that one and only one `Password Policy` can be defined for a particular system under development. For the `Expiration` date, a `group` feature is created. A `group` feature has a set of `grouped` features. In this example, the `Expiration` date has two `grouped` features, `inDays` and `Never`. Thus, passwords can be set to expire after a given number of days, or never expire. The number of days a password remains valid can be set in an integer attribute associated to the inDays feature. The constraints on the number of policies for the Expiration date are captured in the cardinality associated with the group feature. In this case, the Expiration date has the cardinality [1..1], which means that one and only one policy for the expiration date can be selected. The feature model also takes into account the possible requirements on the characters to be used in a password. The constraints on characters required in a password are specified by a group feature, Chars, with cardinality [1..2]. This means that any actual password policy must specify between one and two requirements on characters (Chars) in a password, Upper Case and/or Lower Case.

Such a feature model can be designed by some specific languages but a convenient way is to use a metamodel to define this language. This aspect is further developed and illustrated in Chapter 3.

2.7. Application engineering

Pohl *et al.* define application engineering as *"the process of SPL engineering in which product line members are built by re-using core assets and exploiting the product line variability"* [POH 05b].

DEFINITION 2.8.– *Application engineering is the process of building the products of the product line and re-using core assets according to the production plan.*

During this process, product designers use the variability identified and the core assets created during domain engineering to ensure the correct derivation of required products. The application engineering process is composed of activities for configuring individual products inside the set of valid variation points (product configuration), and creating product line members by using the available core assets (product derivation). When a product is being produced, the management process has to evaluate whether it is a new product or a product in the scope. If the product is not covered by the scope, the normal strategy is to review the domain engineering to extend the scope and to review the production plan; this is a reactive process. However, in some cases, a lightweight approach is possible where the application engineering becomes a complete software process, as in solution-oriented product lines. It consists of analyzing the new requirements, building the needed assets, re-using some artifacts from the core assets, and composing – all trying to conform to the production plan. This has the drawback of not capitalizing on the core assets and on the domain scope.

2.7.1. *Product configuration*

In SPL engineering, during the product configuration activity, product designers are responsible for configuring particular product line members by choosing sets of valid combinations of variants identified at the domain engineering process.

DEFINITION 2.9. – *Product configuration is the process of selecting a valid and complete set of variants to bind to the variation points.*

In order to build a product, the product designer selects the variants to include in his product. Some variants may be incompatible, some others may have requirement constraints that need to be satisfied, and finally, the set of selected variants should define a viable product. Thus, this process needs some validation steps and also tools to assist in the configuration and validation. Some tools already incorporate feature model design, validation, and verification, such as pure variants [PUR 10]. However, there is a recent and active research area and useful techniques should be transferred from academic to commercial and publicly available tools.

The interested reader can look at our related work in Chapter 8. When product designers select variants to appear in a particular *product configuration* is called *binding time of the variability* [BAC 03, BOS 02, POH 05b]. Some authors have identified the advantages of deciding very late on the binding time, and, thus, making the binding time variable [OMM 02, CZA 05, ASI 07]. The advantage of postponing the binding time is that decisions, i.e. design or technological decisions, may be left open very late in the configuration and derivation processes. This adds flexibility to the product line and decouples platform decisions from design decisions or functional requirements.

Product configuration is a simple task when only considering basic feature modeling. However, it becomes tricky with new feature models allowing cardinality, groups, and constraints. One problem is the volume of the information to manage, but maybe the most crucial issue is to define inconsistent configurations. Product *configurators* are artifacts defined to support the creation of product configurations. The basic functionality of a configurator is to facilitate the creation of valid configurations from given variability models. According to Asikainen *et al.* *"a configurator must make deductions based on the requirements the product designer has entered so far, and prevents or discourages the designer from making incompatible choices"* [ASI 07]. Different configurators have been proposed to support product configuration at different stages of the activity, e.g. [ASI 07, ANT 04, WAG 05, POH 06b]. One example of a product configurator using feature models is the *FeaturePlugin* [ANT 04], a feature modeling plug-in for the Eclipse Platform. The tool supports configuration based on feature models that conform to Czarnecki *et al.*'s feature metamodel from Figure 3.3. This configurator implements *cardinality-based* feature modeling, which includes feature and group cardinalities, and feature attributes. In Chapter 6 we present the product configurator we created to support our MD-SPL approach.

2.7.2. *Product derivation*

DEFINITION 2.10. – *The product derivation is the activity related to the manual or automated construction of product line members from the product configuration, the core asset, and the production plan.*

The requirement specifications of products, which are captured in product configurations, are the main input for the product derivation activity. Therefore, to derive products, it is necessary to *adapt* and *assemble* core assets according to the variants chosen from the variability models and captured in product configurations. The guidelines and rules to build the correct product from a product configuration and the core assets are defined in the production plan. As already mentioned, the production plan refers to a reference architecture, which is the general map to construct the products.

Core assets are, thus, the re-usable artifacts considered as building blocks; these artifacts include re-usable common models, components, documentation, requirements, and test cases among others. Product line architects create core assets according to the variants identified and documented during the activity of variability management. For instance, for the Expiration feature from Figure 2.6, a product line architect creates two (different) software components, one for each group, inDays and Never. The first software component has services for checking that passwords are changed once in a specified number of days, and for supporting the requirement of changing a password. This software component is created for the inDays feature. The second software component, created for the Never feature, only has one service to inform that passwords cannot be changed.

In practice, there is a significant gap between variability at a conceptual level (variation points and variants) and variability at the implementation level (concrete core assets). *Decision models* [ATK 00, BAY 00, FOR 08, DHU 08] intend to close that gap. A decision model is defined as a model that captures variability in a product line in terms of *open decisions* and *possible resolutions* [BAY 00].

DEFINITION 2.11.– *A decision model is an artifact capturing product line variability and making the resolution of this variability effective during product derivation.*

Each decision is expressed in terms of a selected variation point and associated with a set of possible resolutions, which in turn, refer to variants of selected variation points. A set of *effects* is associated with each possible resolution. An effect indicates how a particular core asset is re-used to create a product line member.

DEFINITION 2.12.– *A resolution model is a decision model instance, which binds variability and defines how to derive one product.*

In resolution models, all decisions must be resolved. As resolutions are related to variants and effects on particular core assets, a resolution model defines a product line member including (1) a subset of variants, (2) the core assets required to derive the required product, and (3) the adaptation that must be performed on the core assets to obtain a product line member.

Table 2.1 presents a decision model example to create an SPL, which includes variants of the security profile from Figure 2.6. This decision model includes only one decision expressed in terms of the variation point Expiration date, which has been created as a FeatureGroup. This decision is associated with two possible resolutions, which in turn, refer to variants from the Expiration date variation point, inDays and Never. One effect is associated with each resolution. Each effect indicates the software components that must be deployed in case a particular resolution is selected. Thus for instance, if a resolution model is created including the resolution "Passwords will expire in a determined number of days", then the `PasswordExpire` component is deployed with the rest of the common components.

Decision	Resolution	Effect
What policy for Password expiration will be used?	Password will expire in a determined number of days	The PasswordExpire component is deployed with the rest of common components.
	Password will never expire.	The PasswordNever Expire component is deployed with the rest of the common components.

Table 2.1. *Example of a textual decision model*

Even when decision models help in the process of creating SPLs, there are still several problems remaining regarding the gap between variability at a conceptual level and variability at the implementation level. These problems are important for us when they are taken into the field of MD-SPL approaches. The use of MDE is a promising technique to assist and automate product derivation. We go deeper into these specific problems in Chapter 4 and Chapter 5.1, which will explicitly deal with such issues.

2.8. Benefits and drawbacks

On the technical and software engineering side, SPLE should improve and rationalize the management of the core assets. We can expect a better quality of the re-usable assets as they are re-used and tested over and over. It also improves the architecture of applications, tracks code duplication, and increases the artifacts re-use. The consistency of all the assets is better since a global view of the architecture and of the products is maintained. Requirement engineering is a mandatory step; it requires strong interactions with the clients, and thus it provides a more stable and organized set of requirements. There are other benefits for the company that adopts the product line approach. It increases the company's domain knowledge and its expertise about the product that it is developing and selling. This also has important business benefits in terms of product costs, time-to-market, and process efficiency. The company can expect some strong feedback on its organization and its relationships with customers becomes more reliable.

Nonetheless, there are also some drawbacks. One of the main drawbacks is that product line engineering needs expertise and an initial investment. It is not realistic to expect a quick return on investment; visible benefits are not immediate since we first have to play domain engineering. It is well known that a sufficient number of products must be developed before the product line takes advantage over a more classic software engineering approach. Due to the efforts to launch SPLE, this is mainly adopted by big companies and is difficult for smaller companies. To manage a product line requires connecting and using various tools and formalisms. It is difficult to make various software systems interoperable. This is a point where MDE is still a promising technology. There are also social resistances, for instance, to change the practices of engineers and developers. Thus, a domain expert is required to correctly manage a product line project but participants should also get a global view of the entire product line. This needs an initial investment for teaching SPLE in the company. Communication and documentation about the product line are important aspects to ensure the global consistency between the various activities and stakeholders.

2.9. Issues in product line

Several issues exist in the adoption of software product lines. Here, we focus on some of them: the use of MDE to automate and represent variability, testing, the need for traceability, software evolution, and tool support.

2.9.1. *Variability management*

At present, there is no standard way to represent variation points and variants in variability models. However, one of the most used methods to represent variation points and variants is by means of feature models. Feature modeling and meta modeling deserve special attention in this book. Currently, in SPL engineering, there is a trend to separate different concerns involved in a product line. For example, it is desirable to create a variability model including software design concerns separately from technological platform concerns. This separation of concerns facilitates the product line architects' tasks focusing on particular concerns at different times. Similarly, when products are configured, staged feature configurations could be created by different groups of product designers focusing on particular concerns. To facilitate the separation of concerns and the staged configuration of products, separate feature models can be created. Czarnecki *et al.* motivate the concept of staged configuration and stepwise specialization of feature models [CZA 05]. They propose to create separate feature models but with relationships between them. Thus, they avoid a breakdown between the different concerns of individual feature models. For instance, they create a feature model including software architectural concerns and another feature model including technological platform concerns. They maintain relationships between these feature models. For example, one relationship indicates that only if the feature *ObservablePattern* of the architectural feature model appears in a feature configuration, then the feature *OSGi-PeriodicComponent* of the platform feature model will be available to be selected. In Chapter 4, we present how we have introduced the concept of staged expression of variability and staged configuration of products in our MD-SPL approach.

2.9.2. *Product derivation*

Product derivation is the process of building a product from its configuration and according to the production plan.

The product derivation follows a complete software lifecycle with re-use of the core assets developed during domain engineering. Engineers aim at automating and increasing software productivity. MDE was already used to improve SPLE and one of its benefits is to make the automation of the production plan possible. However, this is a complex task, which needs several stages and various kinds of artifacts. Variability can occur everywhere. Given that one objective of SPLE is to automate the process of deriving products, there exists the need for using mechanisms that allow designers to automatically select and assemble the common core assets and variable core assets, which are assets related to variants (features). These mechanisms must also ensure the *correct* assembling. By *correct*, we mean assembling the required configured product. Therefore, an open issue is the definition of explicit models to capture (1) the relationships between features and core assets, and (2) the required rules to assemble them to create valid products based on product configurations.

2.9.3. *Testing*

In the context of SPLE, we must revisit the testing practices since they raise new challenges. In [PM 06a], Pohl and Metzger summarize the three main points. The first is about what to test during the two engineering steps. We could test the commonalities and the different variants. However, separately, they cannot define a viable product. Another problem is that the number of product combinations is exploding; thus, it is not feasible to test all of them. We need to test the realized products and we expect to re-use the tests done for other products sharing the same concerns or features. One rule seems to define the tests accordingly with the variability; in some sense, the tests are new products defined during domain testing and built in application testing. The last point is related to the variability binding in a product. Two problems occur. In the first, a feature is not bound in the product, but it should be present. The second problem is the opposite: a variant has been selected but the configuration choice would have to eliminate it. Testing the commonalities is mandatory, but testing the most used variants in the products could be critical. Thus, it is a good practice to test the reference or base application intensively and to elaborate a plan for re-using testing artifacts.

2.9.4. *Traceability*

Traceability means to follow the life and the dependencies of the artifacts in the development cycle with the software evolution. Traceability is a necessary system characteristic; for example, to support software management, change impact analysis, software evolution, and validation. Providing traceability support during product line development is a complex feature since it concerns every artifact, every development step or iteration, configuration, and evolution management. Traditionally, links between artifacts of a single development step are called vertical traceability, and links between artifacts of two or more development steps are called horizontal traceability. However, SPLE introduces two new dimensions [ANQ 09] into the field of traceability. The first dimension is traceability of *variations*, which goes from domain engineering to application engineering level. The second dimension is related to configuration management and software evolution, which carries a notion of *traceability in time*. This means that the software product line process has to be modeled, artifacts have to be extended to cope with tracing, and a traceability tool chain needs to be designed and implemented.

Traceability is needed for various purposes and at various levels of granularity. We can expect to trace some parts of the general software process and in case of problems to generate finer trace sets. This is difficult to achieve when the process is only manual. We should collect as much information as possible. A challenge is the management of a huge amount of complex data, which requires a good data base and an efficient querying system. In case of automatic processes, the situation is much better since we can replay the sequence and tune the trace configuration. Traceability is often used for change impact and covering analysis. It is more complex with SPLE since one modification has an effect on re-usable artifacts, than on several products. This holds good for other analysis like covering. The use of MDE to model trace links seems obvious, it provides automation, and can capture links during the tool chain. However, it could also permit the tuning of the granularity of artifacts and the granularity of links needed for a successful analysis of trace links.

As a result, a traceability framework has to be configured for each use by the software architect. The architect has to choose the kinds of artifacts he wants to trace, the dependency links he needs to observe, and also insert the correct trace actions in the right places. Such a framework provides the basic support for storing the chosen artifacts and dependencies using interface managers. In addition, it is possible to provide some interactive help for inserting trace actions in the source code. The interested reader could look at the proposal described in [ANQ 09].

2.9.5. *Product line evolution*

Software evolution is defined as software artifacts evolving over time due to updates and changes during software maintenance. The reasons to maintain software assets are usually classified into four categories: corrective, perfective, preventive, and adaptive. Change in one asset may impact several other dependent artifacts and also several products and probably several versions of the products. Thus, evolution, anticipated or not, is an important challenge in the management of a product line. Analyzing the reasons for changes and the direction of these changes can greatly help in anticipating the evolution. [McG 03] analyzes how evolutionary changes affect the various types of assets in a software product line and how anticipation and direction can save the product line consistency. Conceptual and automated techniques that support these practices are also presented. One obvious link is generally between management of evolution and traceability; both have a common objective of facilitating changes. However, both are very often disconnected and insufficient to manage a product line properly.

In [MOH 08] the authors argue for a strong synergy between software configuration management and traceability repositories. Software configuration management, such as Subversion, or Microsoft Visual SourceSafe are able to store software artifacts and to memorize their evolution. The primary aspect of traceability that is enabled by configuration management systems is the traceability of the evolution of versioned items. As configuration management typically has its own repository and rules to store artifact versions, the difficulty is to facilitate a consistent trace and configuration repository without loss of efficiency, loss of information, or difficult querying.

As far as we know, two attempts have been made to connect configuration management and traceability. An advanced solution is proposed in [MIT 08] with the concept of feature-driven versioning. This is a solution able to version product line artifacts on a per feature basis; thus, it is really adequate for a product line. However, the current configuration management is file based and, thus, it requires a new configuration system. The second approach is described in [ANQ 09, RAS 11]. The solution adopted is to import references of the versioning items of the configuration management repository (SVN in this case) as traceable artifacts. Versioning in the configuration management repository leads to traces in the traceability repository between the considered artifacts. This provides a uniform way to manage and query trace information. One interesting point of this solution is that, once the versioning has been done (automatically or manually), then the traces are automatically created.

2.9.6. *Tool support*

As in general engineering, software engineering needs tool support. These tools can be heterogeneous and interoperable, or they can be well-integrated in an IDE. These tools should support all the steps of the lifecycle and an iterative development process. SPLE adds more challenges since it covers two complete engineering processes. Requirements engineering can be connected with domain analysis; requirements should be structured and organized in a variability model.

Verification and validation of requirements engineering is important to increase reliability and suitability of software systems. Feature model verification and validation is a recent and active area of research; important progress has been made in this context. For example, the ArborCraft tool from the AMPLE project is devoted to assist requirement analysis and to generate a feature model. Several tools already integrate some verifications of the feature model; for instance pure variants. The Feature Modeling Plug-in (FMP) [ANT 04] is a rich diagrammatic notation with cardinality, group, and constraints. It already allows a static verification of the feature model and checking of the constraints for a configuration. SPLE also requires expression of variabilities and product configurations and verification that it is a complete and consistent assembly. As quoted in Chapter 8, the issues are numerous, but some new techniques are emerging.

The core assets is a repository that should be managed and browsed. To explore the core assets means to search for a given piece of software and re-using it as such or after some customizations. One difficulty is that artifacts are evolving; a versioning and software configuration management system should be used. New domain specific languages are required in order to represent the production plan and the reference architecture. The automation of product derivation is a promising issue. Since the reference architecture and product configuration are software pieces, the next step is to add generative power to it. Elaborating a partially automated production tool chain is an important challenge for efficiency and code quality. Traceability support demands specific tools that support all the dimensions [ANQ 09].

Product-line testing is crucial to success in SPLE. For test automation, the "Tool Support" practice area in the Framework for Software Product Line Practice developed by the SEI provides a comprehensive discussion. However, concrete mechanisms for testing of product lines and tools to support those mechanisms are subjects that need greater emphasis in practical approaches. There are still fundamental challenges in tool support for testing SPLs. For instance, how can we manage the complexity of the test space taking into account possible combinations of several variants; how can we plan, manage, and execute different types of testing such as unit testing, integration testing, conformance testing, and regression testing, using SPL-driven tools. Recurrent solutions provide a configuration management tool to manage multiple versions of each test. This strategy can be used to provide traceability between the tests and the artifacts to which they are applied. Then, SPLE tests can be taken from repositories and parameterized based on the variation points captured in variability models. This solution has some strengths and weaknesses. That is why these subjects are still open for discussion and are the motivation for events such as the series of International Workshops on Software Product Line Testing.

2.10. Summary

Software product line engineering is a recent trend in software development. It can bring benefits in terms of costs and productivity; however, it also involves a complex software development process. Many software companies are building applications that share more commonalities than differences. They often repeatedly add new features and build new variants or releases of their applications. Most often, software development consists of creating variations from existing software. The strategy of the planned re-use of software artifacts promoted by SPLE has been seen as a means to alleviate problems associated with software development. The SPLE has a two-fold software process: domain engineering and application engineering. These two processes are also often called "development for re-use" and "development with re-use". Domain engineering is responsible for analyzing and modeling the variability in product lines. It also builds the core assets and defines the production plan. The variability model is a structured representation of the commonality and the variability of the products in the scope of the line. One of the main notations is feature modeling; however, metamodels are used more and more to represent variability. Application engineering is the process of creating a product from the product configuration and the core assets following the production plan. Product configuration is an assembly of variants binding the variation points defined in the variability model. Benefits of a product line are clear, provided that the initial investment was precisely measured. Engineers do not have to minimize the complexity and the organization needed to successfully launch and manage a software product line. There are still numerous issues in SPLE: variability management, product derivation, core assets exploitation, testing, traceability, and tool support are some concerns we discuss in this book.

Chapter 3

Model-Driven Engineering

3.1. Introduction

The use of abstract descriptions of systems before building a complex system is mandatory in every engineering and modern discipline. Today, no one can imagine building a system without a extensive analysis of its overall organization, the interactions between its parts, the cost of building the system, the study of properties such as security or robustness, and so on. Models, architectures, or plans are used to design complex systems in general engineering and model-driven engineering. MDE proposes a framework using models as first engineering artifacts to define software development methodologies, to develop systems at any level of abstraction, and to organize and automate system testing and validation. Thus, MDE conceives the whole software development cycle as a process of creation, iterative refinement, and integration of models. During the software lifecycle, stakeholders create models and use model transformations to derive products.

MDE expectations are to increase software productivity by simplifying and automating the design and promoting communication between stakeholders and teams working on the system. One of the main reasons for the attractive power of MDE is its ability to address the entire software development process (requirements, architecture, coding, testing, and traceability) in an iterative view well suited to modern software lifecycles. This trend allows designers to specify software using platform-independent descriptions called models. These models are then gradually (manually or automatically) transformed into executable applications for different platforms and targeted devices. Models help us in understanding, building, verifying, maintaining, and documenting software systems. MDE shares with more traditional compilation techniques, or "the gammarware way", some concerns such as abstraction, early verification, and automatic code generation.

This chapter presents the main concepts involved in the MDE paradigm: models, metamodels and model transformations. It also briefly introduces the object constraint language (OCL), a valuable tool to complement structural model descriptions. Additionally, this chapter introduces some representative modeling frameworks and model transformation languages. These MDE-frameworks and the transformation languages provide specific functionality to create and process models based on the MDE principles.

3.2. Models and metamodels

MDE uses models as first-class entities during the whole software development process. There is no standard definition of a model, even in the software engineering field. There is, however, a common consensus among many definitions about one fundamental characteristic: a model is an abstraction of a system and/or its environment. The MDA guide [OMG 03] defines a model of a system as follows: "*A model of a system is a description or specification of that system and its environment for some certain purpose*".

A model has been usually referred to in software engineering as an artifact built by using a modeling language (e.g. UML). Stachowiak [STA 73] describes the model concept more precisely by presenting three criteria, which were also discussed by Kuhne [KÜH 05]:

– *Mapping. A model represents a mapping between some part of the reality and the set of elements forming the model*;

– *Reduction. A model only reflects a (relevant) selection of the original's properties*;

– *Pragmatic. A model needs to be usable in place of the original with respect to some purpose.*

A model is specified in some modeling language. Modeling languages are usually called domain specific modeling languages (DSML) because they are tailored to certain concerns of specific domains, which make them easier to specify, understand, and maintain than general-purpose modeling languages. DSMLs tend to support high-level abstractions, which are closer to the problem domain than to the implementation domain.

A DSML is either visual or textual and involves at least four aspects: (1) a notation for the construction of models, which is defined by a *concrete syntax*, (2) a description of the vocabulary (concepts, relationships, and integrity constraints) of the domain concepts, which is defined by an *abstract syntax*, (3) *mappings between abstract and concrete syntax*, and (4) the way to use the domain concepts to create well-formed models, which is defined by the *semantic domain*. The semantic domain is usually defined by means of some mathematical formalism in terms of which the meaning of the models is explained [EME 04]. This is a form of static semantics for models. The dynamic semantic is a more difficult thing to express; formal or mathematical notations are required. In the context of UML and MDE, it is often defined using OCL expressions, see section 3.3.

Figure 3.1 presents a model example. This is a class model. The concrete syntax we used to create this model presents model elements as stereotyped boxes and labeled arrows. Each stereotype in a box indicates the type of model element. Values for element properties are displayed inside each box. Relationships between model elements are represented by standard class model arrows (directed-composition or directed-association arrows). Thus, the class model has one package, School, containing two classes, Student and Program. Student has two attributes, studentName of type String and registeredProgram of type Program. Program has one attribute, programName, which is of type String. The composition links from the package named School and the two classes (Program and Student) are labeled with their roles, respectively class1 and class2.

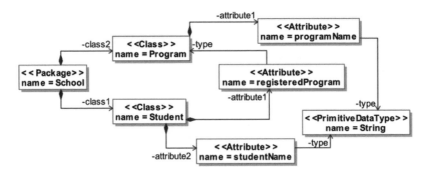

Figure 3.1. *Class model example*

The abstract syntax of a language is often defined using a metamodel. A metamodel describes the concepts of the language, the relationships between them, and the structuring rules that constrain the model elements and their combinations to respect the domain rules. Figure 3.2 presents a sample metamodel for UML class models. This metamodel is expressed as a UML class diagram and includes the metaconcept of Classifier, which is the abstract superclass of both the concrete metaconcepts PrimitiveDataType and Class.

A `Package` is composed of `classes`, and a `Class` contains attributes.

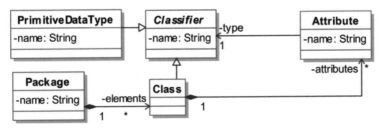

Figure 3.2. *Metamodel for class models*

The relation between a model and its reference metamodel is called conformance [BÉZ 05]. Thus, we say that a model *conforms* to its metamodel, i.e. a model is written in the language defined by its metamodel. The relation of conformance is a mapping between the data of the model type and the model instance. There is, first, a notion of structural conformance that intuitively means that each element in the model is a valid instance of its type in the metamodel. This is true for objects, associations, inheritance, and other links. Since the metamodel can also express constraints, a model must also satisfy the cardinality, or other first-order sentences expressed by these constraints. These notions are not usually well understood by users; however, recent work has successfully defined them. In [EGE 09], the authors propose formal definitions for the notions of structural conformance and semantic conformance in order-sorted logic. Furthermore these semantics can be automatically checked by OCL tools. According to our model and metamodel example, Figure 3.1 presents a class model that conforms to the metamodel for class models in Figure 3.2. The mappings between abstract and concrete syntax can be seen in the stereotypes presented in Figure 3.1, where boxes have the stereotype that correspond to metaconcepts.

Another metamodel example, in the context of this book, is Czarnecki *et al.'s* metamodel, which is the reference model to create feature models such as those presented in Chapter 2. Figure 3.3 presents Czarnecki *et al.'s* feature metamodel [CZA 04]. FeatureGroup expresses a choice over the set of GroupedFeatures in the group and its groupCardinality defines the restriction on the number of choices. A GroupedFeature does not have cardinality and a SolitaryFeature is a feature that is not grouped by any FeatureGroup. The cardinality of a SolitaryFeature specifies the maximum number of times this feature can appear in a final feature configuration. Thus, for example, if a SolitaryFeature has cardinality [1..2], this feature can appear once or twice in a feature configuration. The process of creating several features in feature configurations from one SolitaryFeature is called *cloning*, and the features created are called *clones*. Finally, features may have Attributes of different types and references (FDReference) to other features. The values for the attributes related to clones can be different for each clone.

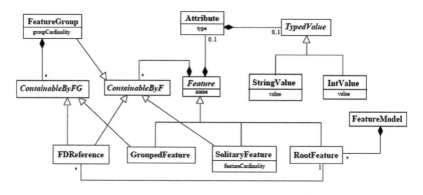

Figure 3.3. *Czarnecki et al.'s feature metamodel [CHE 04]*

Figure 3.4 presents our Smart-Home feature model for the facilities introduced in Chapter 2. One FeatureGroup appears for each group of facilities. The Lock Door Control feature groups the features Fingerprint and Keypad and has cardinality [0..1], which means that Door elements can have either keypad, fingerprint, or none of them as a lock door control mechanism. The `Environmental Control` feature groups the features `Air Conditioning` and `Automatic Windows` and also has cardinality `[0..1]`, which *implicitly* means that `Room` elements can have either automatic windows, air conditioning, or none of them as lock environmental control mechanism.

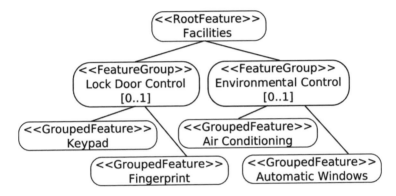

Figure 3.4. *Smart-Homes' facilities feature model*

3.2.1. *The 4-level metamodeling framework*

Since metamodels are also models, they need to be written in another language, which is described by its meta-metamodel. This recursive definition normally ends at that level, since meta-metamodels conform to themselves [BÉZ 05, OMG 06B].

The OMG has introduced the Meta Object Facility (MOF), a 4-level metamodeling framework that removes ambiguities from the term *meta* [OMG 06B]. MOF can be seen as a DSML for defining metamodels; in other words, a standard for writing metamodels. The OMG framework is based on a four-layer metadata architecture used to describe the relationships between data and descriptions of them. These layers are `Information`, `Model`, `Metamodel`, and `Metametamodel`. The `Information` layer comprises the data to be described. The `Model` layer contains metadata that describes the data in the information layer. The `Metamodel` layer is composed of descriptions that define the structure and semantics of metadata. The `MetaMetamodel` layer is composed of the descriptions of the structure and semantics of meta-metadata. Figure 3.5 presents the four-layer metadata architecture.

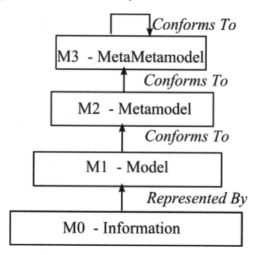

Figure 3.5. *The four-layer metadata architecture*

As defined in its specification V2.0, MOF provides, among others, the following four basic meta-metaconcepts for creating metamodels:

– `Classes` are types. Metaconcepts that conform to `Class` have identity, state, and behavior. The state of a `Class` metaconcept is expressed by its `Attributes` and `Constants`, and its behavior is governed by `Operations` and `Exceptions`;

– `Associations` describe the binary relationships between classes. They may express composite or non-composite aggregation semantics. MOF associations have no object identity;

– `Packages` are containers for modularizing and partitioning metamodels into logical sub-units. Generally, a non-nested package contains all of the elements of a metamodel and packages can be nested to logically organize the units of information;

– constraints specify the well-formedness rules that govern valid domain models. MOF provides several features for metamodel composition, extension, and re-use, including `Class` inheritance, `Package` inheritance, `Class` importation, and `Package` importation.

As part of our work, we have used Ecore as meta-metamodel. Ecore is a core subset of the MOF meta-metamodel where concepts are prefixed by the letter "E". Figure 3.12 presents a part of the Ecore metamodel. As with MOF, `EClass` instances are types. Metaconcepts that conform to `EClass` have identity, state, and behavior. The state of an `EClass` metaconcept is expressed by its `EAttributes` and `EReferences`. Ecore and the Eclipse Modeling Framework (EMF) [BUD 03], which is a framework that aims to follow the MOF standard and uses Ecore as meta-metamodel, are explained in detail in section 3.5.

3.2.2. *The nature of models*

An intrinsic characteristic of MDE is the separation of concerns of a software system into different models. In MDE, it is possible to create and process several models from the same system simultaneously, describing different perspectives or points of view of different stakeholders.

The models describing a system can be classified in terms of their *level of abstraction*. The level of abstraction of a model refers to the extent of implementation details that the model has. In other words, it indicates how close the model is to the problem space; the closer to the problem space, the higher the level of abstraction; the closer to the solution space, the lower the level of abstraction. For example, stakeholders may create high-level abstraction models that include only domain-specific application details or only concepts regarding the problem. Other stakeholders may create or interact with models including details of software design. These models can be considered as medium-level abstraction models.

Finally, stakeholders could process models including details of the technological platforms used to implement the system. These models are considered low-level abstraction models. Thus, MDE conceives software development as a chain of modifications (enhancements) where models of a system are transformed through different levels of abstraction starting at the problem space and finishing at the solution space.

The model presented before in Figure 3.1 is an example of a high-level abstraction model including only concepts regarding the problem space. Figure 3.6 presents a lower-level abstraction model. This model includes software design concerns to represent EJBSession and EJBEntity elements. Thus, this model is closer to the solution space, i.e. it includes more implementation details than the model presented in Figure 3.1.

Figure 3.6. *Low-level abstraction class model*

The separation of concerns of a system in different models according to the level of abstraction is only one of the criteria that stakeholders can use to separate models. At each different level of abstraction of a system, different stakeholders may have different points of view of the system. Figure 3.7 presents an example of a high-level class model including an extra property, isPersistent, related to Class elements. This property allows stakeholders to tag the Class elements whose data need to be maintained in a data base repository.

3.3. UML class diagrams and OCL

In the previous sections, we saw how to describe models and metamodels using structural descriptions inspired from the so-called class diagram of UML. However, as for UML, structural descriptions alone are not sufficient to precisely describe the information. The object constraint language (OCL) is a purely functional language (that is side effect-free) and OOP style devoted to the description of UML elements and navigation in diagrams. It was originally developed by IBM in 1997 as a formal specification language for UML. Now, it is a part of the UML standard and may be used with any MOF metamodel, including all UML diagrams. The OCL 1.4 definition specified a constraint language and OCL 2.0 has been extended to include general object query language definitions. OCL is based on first-order predicate logic and uses syntax close to programming languages and related to the syntax of UML. It is more suitable for everyday modeling than pure first-order predicate logic.

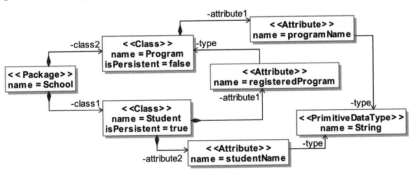

Figure 3.7. *Class model with persistence's properties*

The reason OCL is used is that some computations cannot be expressed solely with diagrammatic notations. For instance, a UML diagram, such as a class diagram, is typically not refined enough to provide all the relevant aspects of a specification. There is then a need to describe additional constraints about the objects in the model. OCL is a formal language to specify unambiguously constraints with no side effects, which means that the states of objects in a model cannot change during the evaluation of OCL sentences. For example, we can represent collections of elements by using class diagrams, but if we want to define sorted lists or lists without duplication we should use some constraints. These constraints can be expressed with OCL sentences; this is the main usage, but it is also useful in expressing the semantics of methods in a pre/post-condition manner. The interested reader could look at the official site http://www.omg.org/spec/OCL/ to find a more detailed and exhaustive presentation of this language. To get a more rigorous insight of it [RIC 02] presents a formal syntax and formal semantics based on set theory for invariant, pre-conditions, and post-conditions.

In OCL, a constraint is written as an expression between brackets (`{}`) and associated with an element in a model, usually inside a comment box. In UML such an expression can denote various things such as structural constraints for classes, semantics of methods, guards in state diagrams, guards with messages in sequence charts, a set of objects and operations on them, or specification of derived elements (attribute, associations). Navigation is done by the usual dot notation (`.`) but more often a navigation denotes a collection of objects, an arrow (`->`) should be used in this case.

A simple expression is to reference an attribute, for instance in Listing 3.1 we state that the name cannot be the empty string. To reference an attribute, it is sufficient to name it: `not(name = "")`. The same notation is used to call a method: `not(name.equals(""))`, provided that `equals` is a method of class `String`. To navigate through an association, the best way is to use its role, if it exists, or else to use the association name or the target class name. For instance, `anAttribute.type.name = "Integer"` should check that the name of the type of `anAttribute` object is equal to `"Integer"`. Generally, such a navigation denotes a collection of objects rather than a single object and we should rely on the `->` operator. For example, `name->isNotEmpty()`, `aPackage.elements->isEmpty()` or `aPackage.elements ->first().attributes->isEmpty()`.

Nevertheless, these expressions should be written in a specific context to avoid ambiguities. A context is either the global context or an element of the considered diagram. The textual notation provides the `context` keyword, but, in addition, we should also define the kind of information. An invariant specifies a property, which must hold at each state of the computation. This is a common property in computer science and it is expressed by the `inv` keyword. A simple invariant for `Attribute` could be `context Attribute inv: not(name = "")`. The context notation must denote the exact element, and sometimes it is required to apply the `::` operator to navigate inside a package or inside a class. For instance, `context foo::bar::Attribute` denotes the class `Attribute` in package `bar` inside the `foo` package. In such a context, as with OOP in a method, it could be useful to reference the receiver object that is denoted by `Self` as in `context Attribute inv: not(Self.name = "Foo")`.

To specify a method is a bit more complex; the first task is to define the name, the parameters, and the resulting type. The keywords `pre` and `post` are related to the description of the pre-conditions and post-conditions (as per the usual Hoare's meaning [HOA 69]). A simple example for a method that checks if the attribute name is equal to some name n is given in Listing 3.1.

```
1  context Attribute :: check (String n): Boolean
2  pre: not( Self.name="")
3  post: result = ( Self.name = n)
```

Listing 3.1. *OCL method behavior*

The keyword `result` denotes the value returned by the method. The meaning of this expression is the following: if the pre-conditions hold (that is the name exists) then after the call to `check` the post-condition is ensured (i.e. the function returns if the name is equal to n or not).

Sometimes, auxiliary variables are required and can be defined using the `let <variable>:<Type> = <request>`

in <expression> construction. For instance, the capitalize method is described in Listing 3.2.

```
1   context Attribute :: capitalize (): String
2   pre : name–>isNotEmpty ()
3   post : let prem : String = name . substring (1 ,2). toUpper () in
4        result = prem . concat (name . substring (2 , name . size ()))
```

Listing 3.2. *OCL description of capitalize*

In this expression, the prem expression is set and stands in the resulting expression. The @pre operator allows the specifier to specify the changes of attribute values before and after a method call. For instance, if one wants to specify a method that adds a suffix to an attribute name, he will write: context Attribute::addSuffix(String t) post: name = name@pre + "_" + t. The expression name@pre stands for the value of name before the call of addSuffix that is at the pre-condition time.

One important aspect of OCL is navigating through associations. Generally, the association name is used or the role name, provided that the association is navigable. The resulting type of such a navigation depends on the cardinality; if it is 1, it is a single object; else, it is a collection. However, it is also possible to add constraints on the end of the association; for instance, to get a Sequence rather than a Set. To reach an association class, or if the association has neither name nor role, the specifier can use the name of the class in lowercase as an implicit role. To navigate from an association class is like navigating from a class.

OCL is a type-checked language allowing type hierarchies and the associated operators to check for types. It also introduces several base types and collections. Base types are standard: Boolean, Integer, String, Real with their natural operators. The abstract root of the collections is Collection and has subclasses: Set, Bag, OrderedSet and

Sequence. These collections manage duplication and ordering of elements in different ways but somewhat similar to generics introduced in Java 5. These are generic collections and they can be nested. OCL provides a set of generic operators to test and convert collections. Normally, to navigate from a collection, one should use the -> operator but it is also meaningful in case of one object only. OCL defines several operations on collections; they are devoted to computing some information like the number of elements, to search in the collection, to extract some subset or to iterate some actions.

As an example, if we want to check that the class names in a package are not empty, we use the "for all" primitive as in Listing 3.3. The forAll is a universal quantification.

```
1  context  Package :: checkClassNames ()
2  post:  result  =  Self . elements −>forAll (not (name= " "))
```

Listing 3.3. *OCL quantification example*

To find that a class with a given name exists in a package, we will write an expression with the collect iterator as in Listing 3.4. Here the collect builds the set of the class names and includes tests if an element is in the set.

```
1  context  Package :: isIn (String  n)
2  post:  result  =  Self . elements −>collect (name)−>includes (n)
```

Listing 3.4. *Collect and test in OCL*

To compute the set of all the attributes of classes in a package, we could use the general iteration mechanism as illustrated in Listing 3.5. The iterate primitive repeats the collect action, to collect the class attributes, over the elements of the collection (Self.elements).

```
1  context  Package :: allAttributes ()
2  post:  result  =  Self . elements −>iterate (x : Set ;  acc : Set  =  Set { }
3                                        |  acc −>collect (x . attributes ))
```

Listing 3.5. *An OCL iteration*

3.4. Model transformations

Model transformation appears to be one of the most useful operations on models. Model transformations are software artifacts that implement algorithms to transform models conforming to source metamodels into either models conforming to target metamodels or source code.

Figure 3.8 presents the scenario of a model transformation with one source model and one target model. Note that (1) each model conforms to its respective metamodel and (2) the model transformation refers to the source and target metamodels. Metamodels are used in model transformation to navigate models by using *transformation rules*. Transformation rules are considered as functions or procedures implementing some transformation step. They are the smallest unit of model transformations [CZA 06]. Finally, a transformation engine is in charge of executing the model transformation on the source model to derive the target model.

Transformations are equivalent to functions and procedures in programming languages, but for models. The source and target metamodels can be seen as the type of the transformation. This analogy is quite complete since there are imperative and purely functional transformations as well as high-order transformations; besides, transformations can be compound.

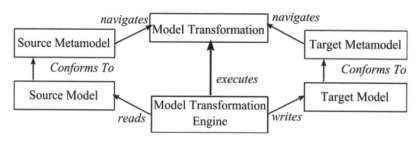

Figure 3.8. *Model transformation scenario*

Listing 3.6 presents an example of a simple declarative model transformation rule using the ATL language [JOU 05]. Line 2 states the source and target models. Line 3 presents the signature of the transformation rule, which creates Table elements (line 7) from Class elements (line 4). Thus, for each class in a SimpleClass model, one table is created in a SimpleRDBMS model. The source and target metamodels (the class metamodel and the RDBMS metamodel) are specified in a descriptor file used to execute the rule.

```
1   module SimpleClass2SimpleRDBMS;
2   create OUT : SimpleRDBMS from IN : SimpleClass;
3   rule Class2Table {
4     from
5       c : SimpleClass!Class
6     to
7       t : SimpleRDBMS!Table (
8           name<–c.name
9       )
10  }
```

Listing 3.6. *Example of a declarative model transformation rule*

```
1   import SimpleClassMetamodel;
2   import SimpleRDBMSMetamodel;
3
4   create Table class2Table(Class c):
5     this.setName(c.name) ->
6     this;
```

Listing 3.7. *Example of an imperative model transformation rule*

Listing 3.7 presents an example of the transformation rule in Listing 3.6 but using Xtend, which is an imperative language [OAW 09]. Line 1 and line 2 present the required import to refer metaconcepts in transformation rules. The rule in line 4 uses a so-called create extension. Create extensions, as a side effect when called, create an instance of the type given after the create keyword. In our case, this rule creates one Table element from one Class element, which is the only parameter. This newly created object can be referred to in the transformation by this (which is why this is specified behind the type). This rule must be called from another rule for each Class element that needs to be transformed.

3.4.1. *Scheduling of transformation rules*

Transformation rules are the smallest units of model transformations. To transform source models into target models, several transformation rules are required as well as an execution ordering. Czarnecky and Helsen name *scheduling of transformation rules* the execution ordering of a set of transformation rules [CZA 06]. Basically the scheduling of transformation rules is a *call graph* in the context of routines to transform models. *A call graph is a directed graph that represents calling relationships between subroutines in a program. Each node represents a procedure and each edge (f, g) indicates that procedure f calls procedure g* [RYD 79]. Describing the scheduling of transformation rules depends on the paradigms followed by the model transformation language chosen to write the transformation rules. Current model transformation languages use well-known paradigms for programming languages. The most common paradigms used in model transformation languages are the *declarative* and the *imperative* paradigms [JOU 05].

In declarative programming, the logic of a computation is expressed without describing its control flow. Model transformation languages applying declarative programming, e.g. ATL [JOU 05] and Tefkat [LAW 07], attempt to minimize or eliminate side effects by describing what the program should accomplish, rather than describing how to do it. For instance, the transformation rule in Listing 3.6 expresses what the transformation does, but it does not provide details about how the transformation is done in terms of cycles, conditionals, and so on.

In imperative programming, computations are described in terms of statements that change a program state. Examples of model transformation languages applying imperative programming are Xtend and Xpand [OAW 09]. Imperative transformation rules define sequences of commands to perform on source models, and require a detailed description of the algorithm to be run and the scheduling of transformation rules. Listing 3.8 presents an example of a detailed description of the algorithm to be run and the scheduling of transformation rules to transform a Class element and its Property elements. In line 6, the rule property2Attribute is called for each Property in the Class being transformed. The rule property2Attribute creates an Attribute and adds it to the collection of attributes of the created Table element (line 11).

```
1   import SimpleClassMetamodel;
2   import SimpleRDBMSMetamodel;
3
4   create Table class2Table(Class c):
5     this.setName(c.name) ->
6     c.properties.property2Attribute(this) ->
7     this;
8
9   create Attribute property2Attribute(Table t, Property p):
10    this.setName(p.name)->
11    t.attributes.add(this)->
12    this;
```

Listing 3.8. *Example of an imperative model transformation rule*

We selected imperative model transformation languages in the implementation of the application examples we used through this book. These are the Xtend and Xpand languages. One of the reasons we selected imperative model transformation languages was to have control on the call graph of transformation rules; thus, we could manipulate it when required. Imperative languages are also easier to learn by most of practitioners who are familiar with OOP; this makes their adoption faster than that of declarative languages.

3.4.2. *Model transformation patterns*

Transformation rules are written in terms of the source and target metamodels. It means that models are transformed following transformation patterns defined in terms of metaconcepts of the source and target metamodels. Figure 3.9 presents an example to illustrate this characteristic of model transformation rules. In the example, Class elements are transformed into Table elements using a transformation rule that is written in terms of the metaconcepts Class and Table.

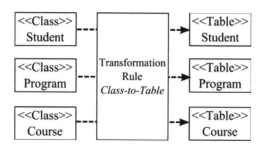

Figure 3.9. *Example of a model transformation pattern*

This characteristic of transformation rules implies that several transformation rules are written when model elements that conform to the same metaconcept are transformed following several (different) transformation patterns. For example, we can write a transformation rule ClassToPersistentClass to transform elements that conform to the Class metaconcept from Figure 3.1 into elements that conform to the Class metaconcept from Figure 3.7, which has a boolean property isPersistent. ClassToPersistentClass transforms any source Class element following a transformation pattern, which creates a target `Class` element with the property `isPersistent` set to `true`. If we need to transform source `Class` elements into a target `Class` element with the property `isPersistent` set to `false`, we must create another transformation rule.

In Chapter 4 we present some mechanisms that allow us to select the transformation rules that must be executed according to particular requirements of stakeholders. For instance, if a stakeholder needs to create a target `Class` element with the property `isPersistent` set to `true`, the rule `ClassToPersistentClass` is automatically selected. These mechanisms also include strategies to modify the scheduling of transformation rules to derive various products.

3.4.3. *Classification of model transformations*

It is possible to classify model transformations according to several criteria. Given the particular interest of our work, we focus on two general classifications. On the one hand, Czarnecky and Helsen have classified model transformations establishing as their major categories model-to-model and model-to-text transformations [CZA 03, CZA 06a]. The reason for this distinction is that the techniques, languages, and tools used for both categories are different. Model-to-model transformations are used to transform models that conform to source metamodels into models that conform to target metamodels. Model-to-text transformations are mostly used for transforming low-level abstraction models into the source code of a specific programming language, and also for generating low-level artifacts including technology implementation details such as deployment descriptors or configuration files. We can also add here the concept of text-to-model transformation denoting procedure used in reverse engineering tools to extract models from code source; for instance, ArgoUML[1] imports

---

1 http://argouml.tigris.org/.

Java or C++ source code and creates the corresponding UML class diagram.

On the other hand, France and Bieman categorize model transformations along vertical and horizontal dimensions [FRA 01]. Vertical transformations occur when a source model is transformed into a target model at a different level of abstraction. A horizontal transformation involves transforming a source model into a target model that is at the same level of abstraction as the source model. The next two subsections deal with these explanations and present some examples.

3.4.4. *Vertical model transformations*

Vertical transformations transform models between different abstraction levels. This type of model transformation is classified in *refinement* and *abstraction* transformations [FRA 01]. Refinement transformations transform models at a higher abstraction level into models at a lower abstraction level, whereas abstraction transformations transform models at a lower abstraction level into models at a higher abstraction level.

Figure 3.10 presents an example of a refinement transformation. On the left, the high-level abstraction model presented before in Figure 3.1 is transformed into the lower-level abstraction model from Figure 3.6. In this example, Package elements are transformed into Model elements and Class elements still remain as Class elements. One Controler element and one View element are created from each Package element and associated with the corresponding Model element. Thus, the target model includes software design concerns to represent a basic Model-View-Controller (MVC) architectural design pattern.

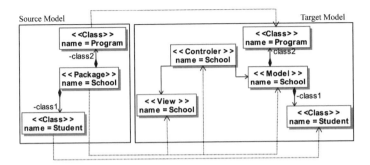

Figure 3.10. *Example of vertical transformation*

3.4.5. *Horizontal model transformations*

Horizontal transformations relate or integrate models covering different aspects or domains within a system, but at the same level of abstraction. Horizontal transformations are classified in *migration*, *merge*, and *identification* transformations [FRA 01]. Migration transformations transform one model that conforms to a source metamodel into another model that conforms to a target metamodel. The source and target metamodels can be the same metamodel. Merge transformations combine individual models, seen as different views, to form a complete model. Finally, identification transformations create target models selecting some elements in source models according to a selection filter.

As part of the approach, we introduce in Chapter 5, vertical (refinement) transformations to incrementally add implementation details to high-level abstraction models until software systems are derived. We use horizontal (*migration and merge*) transformations for adding various concerns to models from the same abstraction level in different model transformation stages.

3.4.6. *Model composition or model weaving*

A simple view of transformation is not sufficient and MDE requires the use of model weaving. The aim is to provide a means to compose models and to represent links between model elements. There are some applications that require this: traceability, model comparison, or model annotation. In these cases, model weaving allows us to capture the links between source and target model elements. This is one point where MDE meets aspect-oriented programming as detailed in [JÉZ 08]. Model composition or model weaving is an operation to combine several models into a single one. A weaving operation is a special type of model transformation that takes two models, M1 and M2, as input and combines their elements into a model M1+M2. Model weaving varies according to composition requirements. Elements to be woven and the way they are combined depends on the required operation. For example, if we compose two class models, it is required to specify what classes from both class models will be in the resulting class model.

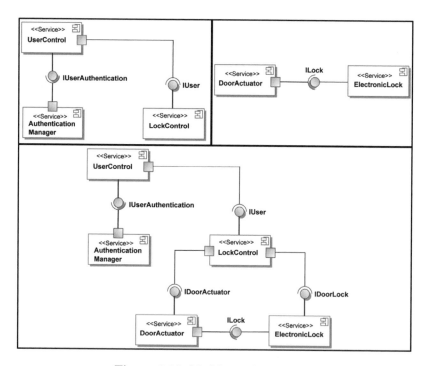

Figure 3.11. *Model weaving example*

Figure 3.11 presents an example where two models that conform to the UML component metamodels are woven. On the left, we present a component model including the components User Control, Authentication Manager, and Lock Control. On the right, we present a component model including the components Door Actuator and Electronic Lock. On the bottom, we present a component model, which is the result of weaving the two models presented before. These models are woven to create an application that automatically opens and closes doors in a Smart-Home.

3.5. Modeling framework

The Eclipse modeling framework (EMF) [BUD 03] is the main academic and industrial reference of modeling frameworks. Other modeling frameworks, such as the Topcased toolkit [PAN 07], extend the facilities that EMF provides. Through our work, we use the Topcased facility to create model editors. This section introduces EMF and Topcased.

3.5.1. *The eclipse modeling framework*

The EMF [BUD 03] is a modeling framework and code generation facility for building tools and other applications based on models. EMF started as an implementation of the MOF specification and currently it uses Ecore as meta-metamodel, which is a core subset of the MOF model.

EMF offers editing tools for creating and manipulating metamodels that conform to Ecore and models that conform to such metamodels. This support includes re-usable classes for building model editors and code generation capabilities. EMF also offers runtime support for operations with models, including change notification, persistence support with XML Metadata Interchange (XMI) serialization, and a reflective API for manipulating EMF objects.

Figure 3.12 presents a subset of the Ecore metamodel. Ecore prefixes an "E" before all its metaclasses. This helps, for example, to distinguish between Ecore metaconcepts and UML metaconcepts. It also makes a distinction between EAttribute and EReference. The difference is that the type of an EAttribute is always a primitive type, such as String or Integer, while the type of an EReference is always an EClass. Associated EReferences are related to each other using the eOpposite property.

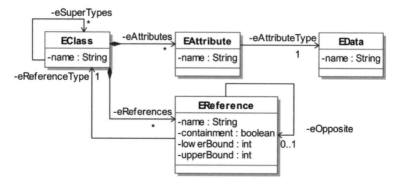

Figure 3.12. *The ecore meta-metamodel*

Ecore models, i.e. metamodels that conform to the Ecore meta-metamodel, can be created in at least three ways: (1) Java Interfaces, (2) UML-type Class Diagrams and (3) XML Schemas. Once a model is created using one of the three different ways, EMF can generate the others. Figure 3.13 presents the EMF editor to create Ecore models using UML-type Class Diagrams. On the left, a sample Ecore model that correspond to a part of the class metamodel shown in Figure 3.2 is presented. On the right, the "palette" of options to create Ecore models is displayed.

EMF also provides facilities to create models that conform to Ecore models; the syntax is based on a tree structure. A tree structure is a way to represent the hierarchical nature of a model. Figure 3.14 presents an example where the EMF model editor is used to create a class model that conforms to the class metamodel. The root of the tree is a package–School. This package contains two classes, Student and Program, which in turn have one attribute each.

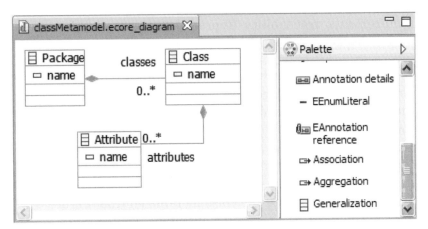

Figure 3.13. *Ecore class model example*

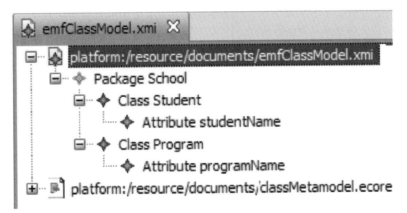

Figure 3.14. *EMF models' editor*

3.5.2. *The Topcased toolkit*

The Toolkit in OPen source for Critical Applications and SystEms Development [PAN 07] (TOPCASED) is an integrated model-oriented system/software engineering toolkit. It covers the stages from requirements analysis to implementation, as well as some transverse activities such as version control and requirements traceability. Topcased provides model editors, model checkers, and model transformations.

Topcased also provides a generative component for developing graphical editors based on Ecore models. Thus, the toolkit allows DSML developers to create and associate concrete syntax to particular metamodels instead of using the general model editor provided by EMF. Figure 3.15 presents an example of a model editor to create class models. On the left, the figure presents the customized palette of options to create models that conform to the class metamodel from Figure 3.13, and, on the right, a class model example.

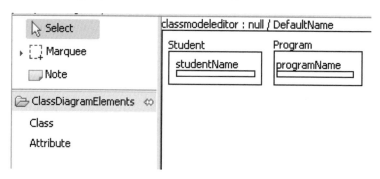

Figure 3.15. *Topcased model editor example*

3.6. Model transformation languages

OMG proposes MOF-QVT (Query/View/Transformation) [OMG 06a] as the standard language for specifying model transformations. QVT exists as an OMG specification; however, even when there are some implementations for the concrete syntax of QVT such as SmartQVT [FRA 09], at the time of writing, there is no official reference implementation.

There are several implemented MOF-based model-to-model transformation languages, such as ATL [JOU 06] and Kermeta [MUL 05]. Similarly, the openArchitectureWare (oAW) framework [OAW 09] provides a textual language to support the activities of model-to-model transformations, the *Xtend* language, but also a language to support the activities of code generation, the *Xpand* language.

3.6.1. *QVT*

Recognizing that model transformations are a critical component of MDE, OMG issued a request for proposal (RFP) in 2002 on MOF Query/View/Transformation. It was finally adopted in July 2007. QVT defines a standard way to transform source models into target models. In QVT, source and target models may conform to arbitrary MOF metamodels. The transformation program is itself considered a model; then, it conforms to a MOF metamodel. This means that the abstract syntax of QVT should conform to a MOF 2.0 metamodel.

The QVT standard only addresses model-to-model transformations. Transformations of type model-to-text or text-to-model, are currently outside the scope of QVT. QVT has a hybrid declarative/imperative nature and it defines three domain-specific languages named *Relations*, *Core* and *Operational Mappings*. Relations is a declarative language, which has a graphical concrete syntax and supports complex object pattern matching and object template creation. Relations supports traces between model elements involved in a transformation (they are created implicitly). Core is a declarative language that supports pattern matching over a flat set of variables by evaluating conditions over those variables against a set of models. In Core, all trace classes are explicitly defined as MOF models, and trace instance creation and deletion is defined in the same way as the creation and deletion of any other object.

The Operational Mappings language is an imperative language that extends both Relations and Core. The syntax of the Operational Mappings language provides constructs commonly found in imperative languages (loops, conditions, etc.). The language provides OCL extensions with side effects that allow a more procedural style, and a concrete syntax that looks familiar to imperative programmers. Operational Mappings can be used to implement one or more relations from a Relations specification when it is difficult to provide a purely declarative specification of how a relation is to be populated. Currently, there are several products that claim compliance to the QVT standard. Smart QVT is the most representative one [FRA 09]. This is an open-source model transformation tool implementing the MOF 2.0 QVT-Operational Mappings that is being developed by France Telecom R&D as an Eclipse plug-in. Listing 3.9 presents an example of a SmartQVT program to transform a class model into an RDBMS model. In line 2, the source model (`srcModel`), source metamodel (`ClassMetamodel`), target model (`destModel`), and target metamodel (`RDBMSMetamodel`) are presented. The `main` (line 3) is the entry point to the transformation. In line 4, `srcModel.objects()[Class]` returns all the elements in `srcModel` that conforms to the `Class` metaconcept. This operation is a shorthand for the OCL-type sentence `select(e | e.oclIsKindOf(UML::Class))`. In line 4, `->` `map class2table()` applies the mapping `class2 table()` to each returned class element. A mapping is an operation associating an element from a model with another element often from another model. In this case, each `Class` element is transformed and associated with a `Table` element. Line 5 transforms the `Association` elements of classes to the `Association` elements of tables.

```
1  transformation Simpleuml_To_Rdb
2  (in srcModel: ClassMetamodel, out dest: RDBMSMetamodel);
3  main() {
4    srcModel.objects()[Class]->map class2table();
5    srcModel.objects()[Association]->map asso2table();
6  }
```

Listing 3.9. *Example of a SmartQVT program*

3.6.2. *ATL*

ATL (ATLAS Transformation Language) is a model transformation language and toolkit currently developed and maintained by the OBEO company and the AtlanMod team. It was initiated by the AtlanMod team (previously called the ATLAS Group) as a part of the AMMA (ATLAS Model Management Architecture) platform. ATL was developed to answer the QVT RFP. The language is specified both as a metamodel and as a textual concrete syntax. ATL transformations are unidirectional, operating on read-only source models, and producing a write-only target model. During the execution of a transformation, only the source model is navigated and changes are not allowed. An ATL transformation program is composed of rules that define how source model elements are matched and navigated to create and initialize the elements of the target models.

Like QVT, ATL is a hybrid transformation language that contains a mixture of declarative and imperative constructs. The preferred style of writing transformation is declarative, which allows the easy expression of simple mappings. Imperative constructs are also provided so that complex mappings can still be specified. The declarative style of transformation is usually based on specifying relations between source and target patterns. This can be seen as closer to the way the MDE developers perceive a transformation. This style stresses on encoding these relations and hides the details related to selection of source elements, rule triggering and ordering, dealing with traceability, etc. Imperative programming makes "native" operation calls possible. This solution moves the control flow out of the transformation language semantics. The operative part of ATL is based on two constructs, (1) called rules and (2) action blocks. A called rule is basically a procedure. An action block is a sequence of imperative statements and can be used instead of or in combination with a target pattern in matched or called rules. The imperative statements available in ATL are the well-known constructs for specifying control flow such as conditions, loops, assignments, etc. The available ATL tools include an ATL transformation engine, an ATL IDE based on Eclipse, and an ATL debugger. Listing 3.6 presents an example of an ATL transformation rule.

3.6.3. *The openArchitectureWare framework*

openArchitectureWare [OAW 09] is an MDE framework integrated recently into Eclipse. oAW offers facilities to transform models into other models or into text or source code. At the core of oAW, there is a workflow engine allowing the definition of model transformation *workflows* by sequencing diverse *workflow components*. A workflow component specifies a step in the model transformation chain. oAW has some pre-built workflow components that facilitate the reading and instantiation of models, checking them for constraint violations, and transforming them into other models or source code. Transformation workflows are built using XML files that describe the steps needed to be executed in a generator run.

Xtend and Xpand, openArchitectureWare's transformation languages, are built up on a common type system and expression language. Therefore, they can operate on models, metamodels and meta-metamodels by using the same syntax. We have selected Xtend and Xpand as our transformation languages and implemented our illustrative examples using and extending oAW. In the following subsections, we introduce oAW, the type system and the expression language used by the Xtend and Xpand languages, and the Xtend language itself. Given that, the Xpand language uses the same type system, the expression language, and the general facilities that Xtend uses. In this section, we do not include a particular description of Xpand. For details, please refer to the oAW manual reference [OAW 09].

oAW provides support for Aspect-Oriented Modeling (AOM) and AOP in the context of MDE. In section 3.6.4, we will illustrate how AOP is integrated into MDE. This characteristic is specially useful to create SPLs using the MDE principles [VÖL 05, GRO 08, VÖL 07a, VÖL 07b], and it is one of the main reasons why we had selected oAW as the implementation framework for our approach.

The oAW type system. In the oAW generator framework, every object (e.g. metaconcepts, model elements, values, etc.) has a type. Every type has a simple name (e.g. String) and an optional namespace used to distinguish between two types with the same name. Thus, a fully qualified name looks like this: `my::fully::qualified::typeName`.

The type system provides access to built-in types such as `String`, `Object`, `Collection`, `List`, or `Set`. Each type contains properties and operations. For instance, the `String` type has a library, which is especially important for code generation. The type system supports the `'+'` operator for concatenation, the usual `java.lang.String` operations and some special operations such as `toFirstUpper()` and `toFirstLower()`.

The type system is also extensible, allowing for accessing types corresponding to models or metamodels created by MDE developers. For example, an MDE developer can register the class metamodel from Figure 3.2 in the type system and then have access to the types `Package`, `Class`, and `Attribute`.

The oAW expression language. The oAW expression language is a syntactical mixture of Java and OCL. For instance, to access a model element property, the following syntax is used: `myModelElement.property`. Respectively, a boolean expression looks like this: `!("textExample".startsWith('t') && ! false)`. The expression language provides several literals for built-in types, for example, the boolean literals are `true` and `false`. Like OCL, the expression language also defines several special operations on collections such as `select`, `collect`, `reject`, `forAll` and `exist` between others. For instance, the `forAll` operation allows specifying a boolean expression, which must be `true` for all objects in a collection in order for the `forAll` operation to return `true`: `collection.forAll (v | boolean-expression-with-v)`. The expression language includes conditional expressions (if and switch expressions), expressions to instantiate new objects (create expressions) and expressions to define local variables (let expressions) among others.

3.6.4. *The Xtend language*

The Xtend language is a textual and functional transformation language. As said before, Xtend is built on the common type system and expression language of oAW. Listing 3.10 presents an example of an Xtend file including transformation rules to transform models that conform to the class metamodel from Figure 3.2 into models that conform to a metamodel of relational database schemas for a relational database management system. The metamodel of the relational database schema has two metaconcepts, `Table` and `Column`. A `Table` contains `columns` and both `Table` and `Column` have a `name` property.

In line 1 and line 2 of Listing 3.10, `import` statements are used to import the name spaces of several types; in this case, the types corresponding to metaconcepts of the `classMetamodel` and the `relationalDatabaseMetamodel`. In line 4, a transformation rule appears. This transformation rule receives one `Class` element as parameter, `myClass`, and returns a `Table` element. As soon as this transformation rule starts its execution, a `Table` element is created. In line 5, the name property of `myClass` is assigned to the name property of the created `Table` element. In line 9, the transformation rule `createColumn(Attribute myAtt, Table myTable)` is called for each attribute of `myClass`. This transformation rule receives an `Attribute` element and a `Table` element, creates a `Column` element from the received attribute, adds it to the collection of attributes of the received `Table` element, and returns the created `Column` element.

```
1  import classMetamodel;
2  import relationalDatabaseMetamodel;
3
4  create Table class2ER (Class myClass):
5      this.setName(myClass.name)->
6      myClass.attributes.createColumn(this)->
7      this;
8
9  create Column createColumn(Attribute myAtt, Table myTable):
10     this.setName(myAtt.name)->
11     myTable.add(this)
12     this;
```

Listing 3.10. *Example of an Xtend model transformation*

In Xtend, a function is evaluated only once for each unique combination of parameters. Thus, one can call the same function with the same number of arguments multiple times, and it will only be evaluated the first time. This is an essential feature when working with graph transformations; especially, if they contain circular references. The Xtend language also provides the possibility to define libraries of independent operations and non-invasive metamodel extensions based on either Java methods or oAW expressions. Those libraries can be referenced from all other textual languages that are based on the expressions framework such as Xpand.

Workflow components. To run the oAW model transformation engine, we have to define a workflow. It controls which steps (loading models, checking and transforming them, generating code, etc.) the engine executes. To transform models into models, Xtend can be invoked within a workflow. An example of a workflow configuration of the Xtend component is presented in Listing 3.11. In line 4 and line 8, the source and target metamodels are registered in the execution context. Thus, the types from the metamodels are added to the set of types available in the type system. In line 11, the root transformation rule, create Table class2ER (Class myClass) is invoked and its result is left in the outputSlot (line 12).

```
1   <component class="oaw.xtend.XtendComponent">
2
3     <metaModel class="oaw.type.emf.EmfMetaModel">
4       <metaModelFile value="classMetamodel.ecore"/>
5     </metamodel>
6
7     <metaModel class="oaw.type.emf.EmfMetaModel">
8       <metaModelFile value="erMetamodel.ecore"/>
9     </metaModel>
10
11    <invoke value="my::path::class2ER(sourceModel)"/>
12    <outputSlot value="transformedErModel"/>
13  </component>
```

Listing 3.11. *Example of a workflow configuration of the Xtend*

Aspect-oriented programming in Xtend. Aspect-oriented programming (AOP) [KIC 97] is a technique that proposes to modularize concerns that crosscut a system decomposition and scatter across multiple design elements. An aspect is a pointcut and an advice. If a pointcut matches some points in the code of an application then the advice is inserted. The process of connecting some aspects on a base code is the weaving process. In the oAW context, aspect orientation is about weaving code into different points inside the call graph of a program. Such points are called *join points*. One specifies on which join points the contributed code should be executed by specifying a *pointcut*, which is a set of join points. Whenever the program execution reaches one of the join points described in the pointcut, a piece of code associated with the pointcut (called *advice*) is executed.

In Xtend, the join points are the invocations to transformation rules. Xtend provides a mechanism to define and use *around advices*. Thus, it is possible to re-use available transformation rules changing part of their behavior without modifying any code.

Listing 3.12 presents an example of an advice, which is weaved around every invocation of the transformation rule createColumn(AttributemyAtt, TablemyTable). This advice is saved as any other Xtend file with extension .ext, for instance myAdvice.ext. Note that the parameters of the transformation rule must be also specified in the pointcut. Inside the advice (line 2), we call the underlying transformation rule. This is done using the implicit variable ctx that provides an operation proceed(), which invokes the underlying transformation rule with the original parameters. Thus, the advice adds an entry to the execution log indicating which underlying transformation rule is invoked, and then it invokes the transformation rule.

```
1  around my::path::createColumn(Attribute myAtt, Table myTable):
2     log("Invoking" + ctx.name) -> ctx.proceed();
```

Listing 3.12. *Example of an Xtend advice*

To weave the defined advice into the selected join points, one needs to configure the XtendComponent indicating the (fully qualified) name of the Xtend file containing the advice. Listing 3.13 presents an example of such a configuration. Note that in line 13, the workflow definition from Listing 3.11 now includes the name of the Xtend file containing the advice.

```
1    <component class="oaw.xtend.XtendComponent">
2
3      <metaModel class="oaw.type.emf.EmfMetaModel">
4        <metaModelFile value="classMetamodel.ecore"/>
5      </metamodel>
6
7      <metaModel class="oaw.type.emf.EmfMetaModel">
8        <metaModelFile value="erMetamodel.ecore"/>
9      </metaModel>
10
11     <invoke value="my::path::class2ER(sourceModel)"/>
12     <outputSlot value="transformedErModel"/>
13     <value="my::Advices::myAdvice"/>
14
15   </component>
```

Listing 3.13. *Example of a workflow configuration including advices*

3.7. Benefits and challenges for SPLE

As seen in Chapter 2, SPLE is a paradigm that focuses on artifact re-use and variability management. It introduces a complex software process with potentially numerous and heterogeneous artifacts. It also requires some specific tasks like product configuration and should put more emphasis on traceability management. MDE appears as a promising technique for SPLE since it provides uniformity and abstraction for software artifacts and processes. The ability to build complex transformations is promising to automate domain and application engineering. However, there are some challenges.

How can domain-specific models help to separate concerns or viewpoints involved in product line development? How do we address domain evolution changes? How can MDE support the process of building product line members from separated models and variability models? For instance, how do we build complete Web applications from independent data models, navigation models, or presentation models? How can models and model weaving help in requirements engineering? How do we use it to structure the concerns and elaborate variability models of a product line?

An important question in SPLE is variability management. The first trend is to use feature models, which express a coarse grained variability grouping set of consistent requirements called features. Another trend, widely used in SPL and MDE, is to have several models capturing different variabilities: domain space, structural models, and technical platform specificities. These models allow a variable-grained approach for variability. Thus, one important question is how to conciliate these different ways to manage variability in a consistent framework? Both have their advantages and seem devoted to different steps of the development cycle.

For domain engineering, the challenge is to build realistic tool chains starting from a feature model and leading to code generation. The designers have to build an adequate representation of the product family at each level. For instance, at the architectural level, the architecture should express all the possible products. It can be viewed as a "super-architecture" superimposing all the products and allowing the selection of a given specific product architecture from the selection of its configuration. The product line reference architecture is the basis for all products and is developed as a creative task. The main approach is to build some template models incorporating annotations that describe what components should be inserted and connected when selecting a feature. Thus, we need to link variation points from a variability model to variants occurring in the products. The tool chain needs several well-defined stages; for instance, domain space modeling with feature model, architecture modeling with UML, and code generation with Java. It is not yet clear which language to use to link variability and variants to allow an automatic derivation mechanism.

For application engineering, two possible uses of MDE are the configuration process and the product derivation process.

The first is about the representation of configuration models; it must cope with the complexity of variability approaches. Feature model configuration is rather simple; however, it is more delicate with metamodels, which allow more powerful and constructive means. The second use is in the derivation process; it should consider the core asset and the configuration model to generate the product. This mechanism should allow the selection of transformation rules and control of their scheduling since there could be some feature or variation interactions.

The complexity of the software process makes the use of traceability to track and analyze the flow of information mandatory. One challenge is the management of a huge amount of complex data. To do a precise analysis, we need relevant data, which means producing and processing this data. We also need a tool supporting most of the stages in a product line, that is, covering end-to-end traceability from market requirements to test cases.

3.8. Summary

The model-driven engineering paradigm organizes the whole software development cycle as a process of creation, iterative refinement, and integration of models. Models are first-class entities that capture a partial view of a system. Each model conforms to its metamodel, which describes the domain grammar and constraints. The unified modeling language is often used to describe the structure of models and metamodels. The object constraint language is the standard language to express constraints over models and metamodels. It is a side effect free and object-oriented language style devoted to the description of UML elements and navigation in diagrams.

Domain-specific modeling is a way to develop software systems that involves the use of domain-specific modeling languages to represent the different concerns of an application domain. In the context of MDE and DSML, we introduce the concept of metamodels, the relation of conformance between models and metamodels, and the MOF 4-level metamodeling framework.

Model transformation appears to be one of the most useful operations on models. Model transformations are software artifacts that implement algorithms to transform models conforming to source metamodels into either models conforming to target metamodels or source code. Transformations can use a declarative or an imperative style. In the latter case, it is important to express the transformation scheduling.

We have explained how MDE uses model transformations to achieve the transition of models between several levels of abstraction by means of vertical transformations. We have also presented horizontal transformations as the mechanism to transform models at the same level of abstraction but integrating several concerns or points of view of an application domain. Model composition and model weaving are more advanced operations on models; this is one point where MDE meets aspect-oriented programming.

MDE technologies are now mature technologies and tool supports are effective. In particular, the Eclipse modeling framework, the Topcased toolkit, and the openArchitectureWare framework are tools enabling metamodeling and automation of model transformation. Model transformation languages still exist as QVT and ATL. We further describe the openArchitectureWare environment since it is used to support our FieSta approach. Xtend and Xpand are the model transformation languages provided by oAW, which also allows aspect-oriented programming in MDE. MDE appears as a promising technique for SPLE since it provides uniformity and abstraction for software artifacts and processes. The ability to build complex transformations is promising to automate domain and application engineering. However, there are some challenges. These will be dealt with in the next chapter.

Chapter 4

Model-Driven and Software Product Line Engineering

Software product line engineering can bring benefits in terms of costs and productivity by taking advantage of the commonality within a set of similar products. These products are adapted during the generation process with variations in their set of features. Positive variability, as one of these processes is referred to, relies on a core set of common features with all products to which additional features will be added. Model-driven engineering techniques and tools have the potential to significantly increase the productivity and quality of software engineering processes. One question that arises is how to integrate these two trends to increment productivity and reduce development costs. That is, how to adapt MDE processes for development of SPLs? How to integrate SPLE for the development of model-driven artifacts? This chapter explores the issues in merging MDE and SPLE to build a production chain to capitalize on product line development, and addresses the main concerns of model-driven and software product line engineering, *MD-SPL* engineering for short. We illustrate the approach by creating our application example of a product line of Smart-Home systems. We include suitable mechanisms to re-use composition techniques from SPLE in the approach, and we merge them with model-driven mechanisms and techniques to capitalize on product line development.

4.1. Introduction

To date, the software engineering industry keeps looking to increase the productivity and quality of software engineering processes, reducing costs, and time-to-market. This is a perpetual challenge; researchers and engineers are focusing on several attempts to improve software engineering practices. However, the industry is struggling to adopt model-driven engineering as well as software product line engineering concepts, techniques, and tools on a large scale as a means to alleviate such needs.

MDE-based SPLs are product lines based on MDE principles. Several approaches that use MDE to create SPLs have emerged. (See Chapter 8 for more details) There is still no standard way to integrate MDE and SPLE, either from a practical or an academic perspective. However, all the current approaches agree that to be successful, model-driven and software product line engineering involves the definition of suitable mechanisms to re-use promised modularization and composition techniques from SPLE. It also involves aligning the academic and practical efforts toward model-driven mechanisms that facilitate the development of software products.

A fundamental objective of introducing MDE in SPL is the expectation of automating the production plan. The ideal situation is to configure products from the set of features or requirements they must include and then to push a button to build the product. However, this ideal situation is far from the state-of-the-art in MDE and SPLE. To fully generate code from models, we need the complete behavior, and it is complex to get structural, functional, and dynamic descriptions together. Generally, models provide structural aspects; some behavioral constraints can be defined using OCL. However, even when OCL facilitates the description of semantics of methods, it does not make the generation of efficient code easier. Some approaches are able to cope with dynamic behavior but consistency of the overall descriptions and code generation remain mainly under study.

Many of the benefits expected from software product lines are based on the assumption that the additional investment in setting up a product line pays off later when products are built. Thus, to define the basis for model-driven and software product line engineering, one must integrate both approaches to define new processes in the *problem space* for expressing variability and configuring products, and in the *solution space* for deriving products. MD-SPL deeply impacts the management of core assets, the expression and use of variability, and the production chain.

Regarding the problem space, the issues are "How to define mechanisms to manage variability based on metamodeling; for e.g. feature modeling? How to implement multi-staged configuration of products? How to model and configure products from several concerns and several abstraction levels?"

An effective return on investment in product line engineering is achievable when the product lines can be efficiently used for product derivation. If we want to improve product derivation, we require models that are more than just vehicles for documentation and discussions on the whiteboard. Then, regarding the mechanisms used in the solution space, questions that arise are: What are the core assets that are required? How to create and use decision models in conjunction with other model assets to tackle the derivation of products?

A general MD-SPL approach can be summarized as in Figure 4.1. We refer to it as the summary of a general MD-SPL approach because the involved processes are used irrespective of the type of product line we are creating: proactive, reactive, or extractive. This view is intended to subsume many other approaches in this domain. One of the first uses of MDE for a product line is the work of Trask in [TRA 06]. It illustrates the importance of domain-specific modeling in the engineering of components and applications for radio. Several approaches to create SPLs have emerged that are based on MDE, such as Czarnecki and Antkiewicz's approach [CA 05], Wagelaar's approach [WAG 05, WAG 08b, WAG 08a], approaches coping with dynamic behaviors [ZIA 06, PER 08], Loughran *et al.*'s approach [LOU, SAN 08], and Voelter and Groher's approach [VÖL 07b]. Recently, the AMPLE way to develop product lines introduced product-oriented and solution oriented approaches and two dedicated MD-SPL organizations. A more detailed discussion about these approaches is provided in Chapter 8.

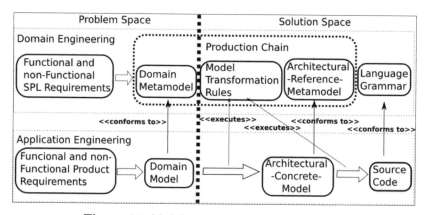

Figure 4.1. *Model-driven software product lines*

The input of any SPL development includes business and non-functional requirements. Both determine the reference architecture, which is depicted by metamodels and model transformations. During domain engineering and problem space, a metamodel of business, the domain metamodel, is created by SPL architects representing the functional scope of the product line. Of course, this design can be complemented using the classic feature model notation. Since metamodels are able to represent the feature model notation, a MDE is general and uniform. Then, from this metamodel, SPL architects develop at least one architectural reference metamodel, which summarizes the architecture of any product line member. Reference architecture captures the common architecture of any product and the variations included in the domain. This design can be complemented using feature models. All the other core assets are created during domain engineering and the production chain is established.

In MD-SPL engineering, the rationale of a production chain is an assembly of model transformation rules that transform domain models into architectural or other intermediate models and finally into source code. The production chain relates three important pieces: the *domain metamodel*, the *model transformation* rules, and the *architecture metamodel*. Obviously, this is the main difficulty in domain engineering since the role of the production chain is to generate a product from a product configuration represented as a domain model, the reference architecture, and other core assets. The production chain is complex and cannot be modeled by one stage only; this is a multi-staged process. Here, we only relate the two main stages and *views*: architecture and source-code levels. Thus, the production chain will first create a product model using model-to-model transformations and then additional model-to-text transformations generate the source code application. Any realistic software engineering chain should be open to the external world, that is mainly to re-use existing artifacts or to support modifications for various evolution purposes. For instance, the use of external libraries can be undertaken both at the architectural or source-code level, provided that component interfaces are well designed and included in the models of the products. Interfaces, in a broad sense, are important artifacts in such types of software chains. Manually written code should, and could, be integrated. Still, interfaces are needed to materialize the contract the programmer has to satisfy during code design.

The notion of views or points of view has been used for a long time in software engineering and is also used in MD-SPL engineering. The development of a complex system needs several stakeholders – requirements analysts, architects, designers, programmers, who are concerned with several different aspects of the software system (requirements, architectures, GUI, persistence, concurrency, security, distribution, etc.). The viewpoints of a software are multiple, and for instance, several approaches have been defined to tackle this issue in OOP [SHI 89, CAR 90]. A reference work for the use of views in architecture is [KRU 95], which distinguishes four views, namely the logical, process, physical, and development views. In SPLE, we deal with traditional views and some new ones. We will use feature models and/or models for variability, a reference architecture, product architectures, component views, technical, or implementation platform information, the production plan, etc. A general software process should start from requirements and lead to source code and testing artifacts. We will present our general view, which is consistent with the one above, but we have not considered requirements analysis. Our process assumes that some requirements are met by feature models and other kinds of models. For a reference that provides a view and tools for requirements analysis in SPLE, the reader could consider [RAS 00]. In the next chapter, we will extend our product line chain to cope with the specific issue of fine-grained variability and configuration. Considering the need for several views, which cannot always be completely orthogonal, models provide a uniform way to represent these various aspects and also the constraints between them. Model weaving and model transformations are the computation processes enabling us to combine these views and to build the full architecture or the full source code. Throughout this chapter, we elaborate the issues involved in integrating MDE and SPLE, and we present our MD-SPL approach, which integrates most of the current MDE and SPLE mechanisms used to build production chains.

4.2. Problem space issues

In the problem space dimension, MDE mechanisms impact mainly on variability expression, the way to configure products, and the elaboration of an automated production chain. The main outcome is that several views of the software are needed, each one with its specific requirements; thus, several stages to define variability and then to configure products are needed. This section describes variability capture based on models and feature models, product configuration, and the concept of multi-staged process.

4.2.1. *Separating points of views*

As discussed previously, the separation of concerns is a mandatory pre-occupation for software engineering. As an MDE approach, an approach to create MD-SPL must define the criteria to decide how to separate concerns from an application domain in several views; this is, how to represent each product line member using diverse points of view, each one including particular concerns. As an example, consider an MD-SPL approach that decides a unique criteria to split the application domain in two separated views: conceptual view and architectural view, which includes details of technological implementation. If we are interested in building our MD-SPL of Smart-Home systems using such an approach, each system should be represented using at least two points of view: the conceptual and the architectural. The conceptual view includes details of functional requirements of the system such as the available rooms and facilities in the house. The architectural view includes, among others, information regarding the type of required software components for periodically checking temperature inside a room.

Decisions on how to separate concerns (how many views to define, how are they related, and so on) are strongly linked to the application domain and the variability identified in the SPL under development. That is why one of the most important characteristics in an MD-SPL approach is that it facilitates and supports the separation of concerns in as many views as required. For instance, the elements concerned with security facilities could be separated if the requirements of the product line demand it. Product designers could then select the security profile for a product line member under configuration. For this, it is mandatory that the MD-SPL approach provide mechanisms for managing several points of view according to the identified variability.

In our application example of Smart-Home systems, we only take into account those points of view related to the architectural structure of buildings, habitat facilities, and software architecture designs. The approach we present in this chapter provides the mechanisms to capture other concerns in separated models if required; for example, views of behavior such as those we can capture with message sequence charts or state charts (see [ZIA 06] for a related approach), or views to capture and express other issues such as performance, distribution, or concurrency.

4.2.2. *Capturing variability and configuring products*

An MD-SPL approach must establish how to represent the several points of view involved with product line members. Metamodeling and feature modeling are the most common mechanisms used in MDE and SPLE, respectively, for capturing and expressing variability. Both metamodeling and feature modeling can be used for capturing not only structural and behavioral variations, but also functional and non-functional requirements. However, they are different in many ways. Metamodels facilitate the modeling of variations at language level. Product designers who are domain experts are capable of configuring different products by creating diverse and rich application domain models. Thus, metamodeling implies a constructive approach that requires a high level of expertise. Still, models and metamodels are general vehicles for expressing variability in software artifacts, which are models in MDE. On the other hand, feature models ease the modeling of variations using a well-known syntax and semantics to capture variability. Feature modeling allows the configuration of products only by selecting features and hiding the complexity of building complex models; this is a selection-based approach that requires only domain knowledge.

The use of alternative (less-used) mechanisms for capturing and expressing variability, such as ontology models from the SPLE field, seems very relevant. However, there are not enough practical examples available to incorporate in the MDE field. Therefore, an MD-SPL approach must provide at least mechanisms to capture variability and configure products based on meta modeling and feature modeling. In addition, the approach must allow product line architects to decide when to choose either metamodeling or feature modeling.

4.2.3. *Relating several points of view*

We introduced the need for MD-SPL approaches for providing mechanisms to represent, using metamodels and/or feature models, each product line member according to different concerns. Thus, a product line architect could, for example, represent the variability of a Smart-Home system by using a metamodel to capture the conceptual elements of the application domain, and by using a feature model to represent the scope of the product line for architectural features. Consequently, a product designer could configure a product by creating a model that conforms to the conceptual metamodel and a feature configuration including architectural decisions.

Nevertheless, an MD-SPL approach must also provide mechanisms to establish relationships between several models. Product line architects have to decide (1) how to separate concerns of an SPL in points of view, and (2) choose the type of models to represent such views. No matter how product line architects decide to separate concerns in diverse points of view, inter-dependencies always remain between several views of a software system. Following the Smart-Home systems example, product line architects must express a relationship between conceptual and architectural elements. For instance, there is a relationship between the concepts representing rooms with automatic windows and the available type of architectural components to implement such a facility.

4.2.4. *Configuring products in a multi-staged process*

MD-SPL approaches should consider several stages for the configuration of products, selecting variants from diverse concerns at each stage. Of course, the relationships between models representing diverse points of view play an important role when products are configured in several stages. It is possible to perform multi-staged configurations only when relationships between models representing variability from the defined points of view are well known and documented.

Using multi-staged configuration, products may be configured at different binding times where at each stage, specific variants are chosen. Multi-staged configuration also facilitates the intervention of product designers with different domain knowledge at different binding times. Then, design or technology decisions may be left open or postponed to the latest possible binding time in the configuration process. Another very important characteristic of multi-staged configuration is that when variants are selected in one stage, variants from the next stage can be delimited because of the current selection.

Figure 4.2 summarizes a process example to configure and derive a Smart-Home system using a multi-staged process. First, a building architect creates a domain model. Then, a facilities designer creates a configuration based on a facilities feature model. Finally, a software designer creates another configuration based on an architectural feature model.

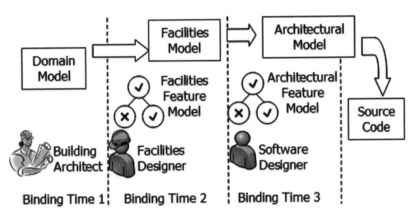

Figure 4.2. *Multi-staged configuration process*

4.3. Solution space issues

The solution space is concerned with the description of a feasible solution to the problem using concrete software patterns and adequate technology. Thus, the main issues concerning the solution space dimension are i) the construction of models, model transformations, textual descriptors, and core assets to implement the variability captured in the problem space, and ii) the design of an automated product derivation dealing with multiple development stages with a range of models and core assets.

4.4. Developing core assets

The development of the core assets is the main stay in SPLE. Some assets are created at problem space to capture variability. Some others are created manually from requirements, by model designers during the transition from problem space to solution space or by programmers who have already implemented re-usable components. In an MDE process, a set of assets is also generated from the transformation steps and they can be subject to re-use. At solution space, some specific assets can be created and subject to re-use in other products.

We summarize the process of deriving MD-SPL as the incremental transformation of application domains models, using re-usable model transformation rules, re-usable models, and re-usable source code to obtain products. Thus, the main core assets used in MD-SPL approaches are models, model-to-model transformations, and model-to-text transformations. Of course, as SPLE approaches, MD-SPL approaches may/must (re-)use, also, pieces of code already developed and well tested.

The challenge of MD-SPL approaches, regarding core assets development, lies in selecting when model transformations, models, or source code must be developed as re-usable core assets. Sometimes, model structures must be built to be used in an intermediate transformation when common models are required. Sometimes model-to-model transformations are required for either (1) transforming source models into target models in some transformation step, or (2) weaving models created by designers or product line architects. Finally, sometimes source code (or any kind of text descriptor) must be developed, tested, and intensively re-used.

4.4.1. *Developing decision models and deriving products*

Given that one objective of MD-SPL approaches is to automate completely the process of transforming models to generate products, there is a need to use a mechanism that allows designers to select and execute transformation rules automatically according to variants selected by product designers through the configuration process. This mechanism must also ensure the correct execution ordering, also called execution scheduling, of the selected transformation rules. By correct, we mean an execution ordering that allows derivation of the required configured product.

There is, then, the need of introducing *decision models* in the context of MD-SPL as a mechanism for composing transformation rules based on product configurations. In section 2.7.2, we presented a decision model as a model that captures variability in a product line in terms of *open decisions* and *possible resolutions* [BAC 00]. Each decision is expressed in terms of a selected variation point and associated with a set of possible resolutions, which in turn refer to variants of selected variation points. A set of *effects* is associated with each possible resolution. An effect indicates how a particular core asset is re-used to create a product line member. Thus, in the context of MD-SPL engineering, decision models must capture (1) the relationships between variants and solution space core assets, such as transformation rules or re-usable source code, and (2) the required execution ordering of transformation rules to weave and transform models and/or source code to create products based on product configurations.

4.5. Variability expression and product configuration

The most common mechanisms used to capture variability and configure products in current MD-SPL approaches are metamodels and feature models. As part of our approach to create MD-SPL, playing the role of product line architects, we use metamodels and feature models as our base core assets. Playing the role of product designers, we configure products by creating (1) models that conform to metamodels and (2) feature configurations.

4.5.1. *Metamodels*

Since we use a multi-staged approach for configuration and derivation of products, we separate domain-specific concepts in several metamodels. To create the product line of Smart-Home systems, the first metamodel we build is the domain metamodel, which serves as a vocabulary that is familiar to the practitioners of the system's domain. A domain model does not include concepts regarding details of the structure or processing of the system. Other metamodels contain facilities and architectural concepts, which are orthogonal to the concepts in the domain metamodel. These concepts represent variability that affects multiple domain concepts and their subsequent processing (i.e. transformation and generation) stages.

Each metamodel has a main objective to capture the variability that characterizes a product line; however, they play different roles during the product line development lifecycle. Product designers use the first metamodel, the domain metamodel, during the configuration process. This metamodel is the reference to create domain models, which are the starting point to derive product line members.

We create four metamodels to capture, separately, the three sources of variability that characterize our Smart-Home system's product line (see Chapter 2):

– *Domain metamodel*. This metamodel includes concepts regarding architectural structure of houses.

– *Smart-Home's facilities metamodel*. Each house may be equipped with several facilities related to controlled devices.

– *Components metamodel*. This metamodel includes only concepts concerning component-based development. This metamodel is important to represent the problem domain in terms of software components.

– Software architecture metamodel. Each Smart-Home system has a technology platform integrating their devices under different software architectures.

It is possible to create other metamodels such as a programming language grammar, or its representation as a metamodel, to capture the final source code of the product line members. In our case study, however, we do not create it; instead, we generate the final representation of a product directly as source code.

The first stage to configure a product starts with the creation of a domain model; i.e. the model that represents a particular building. Figure 4.3 presents the transformation steps of a domain model from its creation until the production of the source code application. The model transformation rules are used in four stages, each one with a dedicated set of rules. The first set of rules is defined from the domain metamodel to the facilities metamodel. The second set is defined from the facilities metamodel to the components metamodel. The third set is defined from the components metamodel to the architecture metamodel. Finally, the fourth set of transformation rules includes model-to-text transformations that produce the source code of product line members. We create model-to-text transformation rules from the facilities and the architecture metamodel to Java source code. The following sections present the details about the model transformations and the possible variations these model transformations can have according to the SPL variability.

We present our four metamodels in detail:

Domain metamodel. The first metamodel is the domain metamodel, which includes application domain concepts that facilitate the creation of models representing the structure of houses. Figure 4.4 presents the domain metamodel. Using this metamodel we can create houses with several architectural structures including several `Floor`, `Room`, `Door`, and `Window` elements.

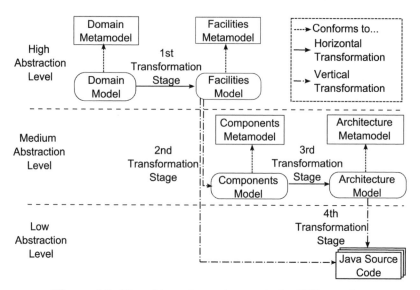

Figure 4.3. *Staged transformations to derive SPL members*

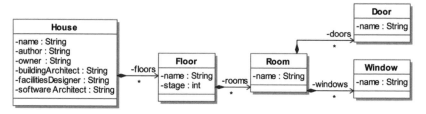

Figure 4.4. *The domain metamodel*

Figure 4.5 shows a domain model example that conforms to the domain metamodel. The model defines `firstFloor` and `secondFloor`. These conform to the `Floor` metaconcept. In the `firstFloor` there are two rooms, `livingRoom`, and `kitchen`. In the `secondFloor` there is another room, `mainRoom`, which has two windows, `mainRoomW1` and `mainRoomW2`. There are also two doors. The first door, `livingRoomD1`, is in the `livingRoom`. The second door, `mainRoomD2`, is in the `mainRoom`.

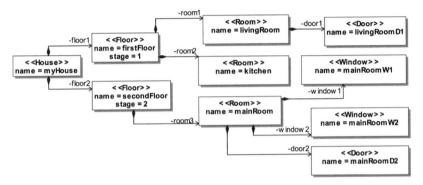

Figure 4.5. *Example of a domain model*

Facilities metamodel. The facilities metamodel is presented in Figure 4.6. This metamodel is at the same level of abstraction as the domain metamodel. The facilities metamodel includes, however, metaconcepts of Smart-Homes facilities, such as environmental control and authentication devices. Based on this metamodel, it is possible to add facilities to Smart-Homes. The `Window` metaconcept is now specialized in `Automatic` and `Manual` metaconcepts. Thus, windows can be configured as automatic or manual windows. The `Room` metaconcept contains one `EnvironmentalControl` metaconcept, which is specialized in the `WindowsController` and `AirConditioning` metaconcepts. Thus, rooms can be configured to manage air conditioning or automatic windows as environmental control. Finally, the `Door` metaconcept contains the `LockDoorControl` metaconcept, which is specialized in the `Fingerprint` and `Keypad` metaconcepts. Thus, doors can be configured to manage fingerprint or keypad as lock door control.

Components metamodel. The software components metamodel is used to represent concepts of component-based development. For instance, in the smart-home, we could have controller components for the windows, the air conditioning, or the door lock controls. We can use several different components technologies such as J2EE and Fractal, but in the domain of home-automation OSGi [OSG 09] is the de facto standard. The chosen technology generally implies a particular metamodel associated with the framework or the language. The interested reader will find general surveys about component programming and architectural description languages in [CZA 99, MED 00]. In our case, we choose OSGi and use a proper metamodel based on UML2 notations. The OSGi framework implements a complete and dynamic component model. Applications or components (*bundles* for deployment) can be remotely installed, started, stopped, updated and uninstalled without requiring a reboot. The management lifecycle is achieved through APIs that allow for remote downloading of management policies. The OSGi metamodel includes more implementation details than the domain metamodel and the facilities metamodel. That is because this metamodel is at a lower abstraction level than the two previously presented metamodels.

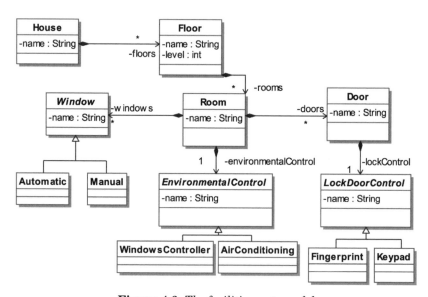

Figure 4.6. *The facilities metamodel*

Figure 4.7 presents our components metamodel. We take the basic concepts from the UML2 metamodel to create a simplified metamodel of components. This metamodel is also a subset of the one developed in the AMPLE project in the context of its Smart-Home case study [AMP 08]. A Component is a modular, replaceable, and deployable piece of software, which interacts with its environment through interfaces or ports [LU 05]. We specialize the Component metaconcepts in the Periodic metaconcept. Thus, we can create Periodic (Component) elements when the component is a periodic component in the final software architecture of a Smart-Home system. A periodic component is an active component whose offered services can be executed periodically according to well-defined business rules. A Port serves as a contract between the elements it connects. Ports are usually of the type Interface. In UML2, interfaces can be either Provided or Required ones. Provided interfaces specify the providedOperations that a component offers to their clients. Required interfaces specify the requiredOperations that a component needs to perform its functions. In UML2 Provided and Required interfaces are related using connectors. To simplify our metamodel, we connect Provided and Required interfaces creating a directed relationship between them, useProvided. Finally, a Component owns a unique identifier, componentName, and a set of Property elements.

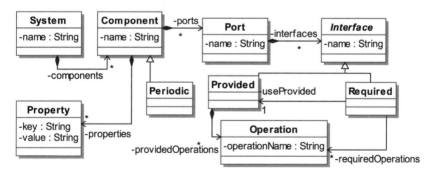

Figure 4.7. *The components metamodel*

The architecture metamodel. The architecture metamodel is at the same level of abstraction as the components metamodel. However, the architecture metamodel includes new metaconcepts to represent the variants identified regarding architectural design. While the components metamodel has general and common concepts regarding component based development, the architecture metamodel refines it to include concepts of specific vendors' implementations such as OSGi. Figure 4.8 presents the architecture metamodel. The Component metaconcept is now also specialized in Service; thus, components can be configured to be either periodic or service components. Furthermore, the Component metaconcept includes the property instantiationMode to indicate when a component is instantiated, ON_INVOCATION or ON_DEPLOYMENT. Thus, a software designer can configure a component to be a periodic or a service component and to be instantiated on invocation or on deployment. Let us suppose a building owner wants to check the environment inside the building to open/close the windows accordingly. Then, the software designer should configure a basic component to manage automatic windows devices to be a periodic component.

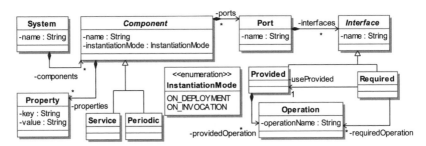

Figure 4.8. *The architecture metamodel*

4.5.2. *Feature models*

Due to the different sources of variability, MD-SPL approaches must allow product designers to configure a product giving its domain model and selecting variants from the sources of variability. For instance, in our application example, those are the variants from Smart-Home's facilities and software architecture. In [POH 05] the authors introduce the idea of an orthogonal variability model dedicated to collecting variability in the entire product line, not only at the level of requirements. This role features models, which address specific aspects of the variability: Smart-Home and building architecture facilities, software architectural considerations, implementation choices, and so on.

Figure 4.9 presents an example of how limited the configuration and the derivation of Smart-Home systems is when only product designers configure a product by means of a specific domain model. In the example, from a building representing the architectural structure of a Smart-Home, only one possible Smart-Home system could be derived, without including variants from concerns different from the structure of the building.

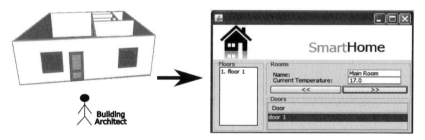

Figure 4.9. *Example of configuration without variability models*

We use feature modeling to allow product designers to configure products from sources other than the application domain. Like metamodeling, feature modeling can be used for capturing not only structural, but also behavioral variations. Metamodeling facilitates the configuration of products by creating rich models using a constructive approach that requires a high level of expertise. Feature modeling facilitates the configuration of products by selecting features and hiding the complexity of building models from scratch; this is a selection-based approach that requires only domain knowledge.

We create our feature models based on Czarnecki *et al.*'s metamodel [CZA 04], which is itself based on FODA [KAN 90]. Figure 4.10 presents our simplified feature metamodel. As in the Czarnecki *et al.*'s metamodel, a FeatureGroup expresses a choice over the set of GroupedFeatures and its cardinality defines the restriction on the number of choices. A GroupedFeature does not have cardinality and a SolitaryFeature is a feature that is not grouped by any FeatureGroup. Examples of feature models are given in the next subsection using our application example.

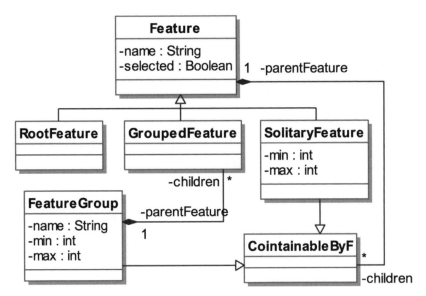

Figure 4.10. *Simplified feature metamodel*

For the SPL of our application example, playing the role of product line architects, we create a feature model that represents variants of Smart-Homes facilities, and another one that represents variants of architectural (software) design. Thus, product designers are able to configure products by creating feature configurations including choices of Smart-Homes facilities and (software) architecture. These feature configurations are input to the product derivation process. They are used to select the transformation rules to be used in each stage of the model transformation chain.

The facilities feature model. As we introduced in section 2, we take into account the need to incorporate to the house, automation facilities that are orthogonal to the house structure. We consider particularly two groups of facilities: access control facilities and environmental control facilities.

Figure 4.11 presents our Smart-Homes facilities feature model. One `FeatureGroup` appears for each group of facilities. The `Lock Door Control` feature groups the features `Fingerprint` and `Keypad` and has cardinality `[0..1]`, which *implicitly* means that `Door` elements can have either keypad, fingerprint, or none of them as lock door control mechanism. The `Environmental Control` feature groups the features `Air Conditioning` and `Automatic Windows` and also has cardinality `[0..1]`, which *implicitly* means that `Room` elements can have either automatic windows, air conditioning, or none of them as lock environmental control mechanism. We say *implicitly* because there is neither semantics in traditional feature models, nor in metamodels, to formally denote that features represent variants that affect particular model elements.

The architecture feature model. Figure 4.12 presents our architecture feature model. Given that we have classified software components according to their type, and their instantiation mode, we create one `FeatureGroup` for each classification. The `Component Type` feature groups the features `Periodic` and `Service` and has cardinality `[1..1]`, which *implicitly* means that `Component` elements can be either periodic or service components. The Instantiation mode feature groups the features Deployment and Invocation and also has a cardinality [1..1], which *implicitly* means that Component elements can be instantiated either on deployment or on invocation.

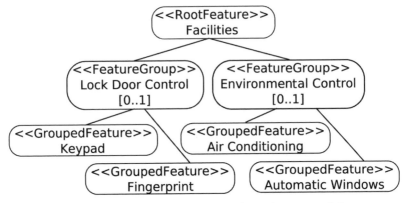

Figure 4.11. *Smart-Homes' facilities feature model*

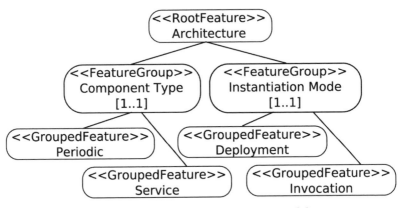

Figure 4.12. *Architecture feature model*

Figure 4.13 summarizes the processes of (1) expressing the variability in our application example SPL and (2) configuring a Smart-Home system, by using only metamodels and feature models. First, a *building architect* creates a Domain Model based on the Domain Metamodel. Then, a *facilities designer* creates a feature configuration based on the facilities feature model. The facilities feature model affects the transformation of the `Domain Model` into the `Facilities Model`. According to selected facilities features, particular transformation rules must be executed to transform domain models into facilities models. For instance, if the feature `Automatic Windows` is selected, a particular transformation rule is executed to transform `Window` elements into `Automatic Windows` elements. If the feature `Automatic Windows` is not selected, another different transformation rule is executed to transform `Window` elements into `Manual Window` elements. The `Facilities Model` is transformed into a `Components model` and then a *software architect* creates another feature configuration based on the architecture feature model. The `Architecture Feature Model Configuration` affects the transformation of the `Components Model` into the `Architectural Model`. Finally, the `Architectural Model` and the `Facilities Model` are used to generate the final `Java Source Code`. The next section describes the process of deriving products using model transformation stages.

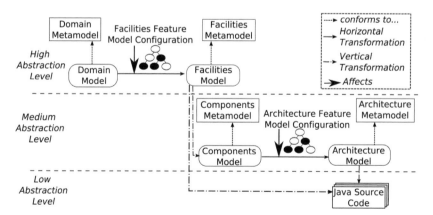

Figure 4.13. *Summary of the Smart-Home systems configuration and derivation process*

Figure 4.14 presents an example of the staged configuration of two different Smart-Home systems. In the example, we only present two stages. In the first stage a building architect configures the architectural structure of a building. In the second one, a facilities designer creates two configurations to derive two different Smart-Home systems from the same building: on the left, the configuration indicates that the Smart-Home system will have a keypad as lock door control in all the doors; on the right, the configuration indicates that the Smart-Home system will have automatic windows as environmental control, which implies that all the windows will be automatic windows.

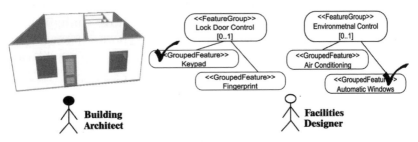

Figure 4.14. *Example of configuration with variability models*

4.6. Core asset development and product derivation

We have introduced metamodels and feature models as the core assets we use in our approach to express variability and configure products. Similar to many other MD-SPL approaches, in our approach, we use model transformation rules as the main core assets to derive product line members. In addition, we also use pre-created software artifacts to assemble final products.

In the next two subsections, we present (1) the transformation rules and software artifacts we have created for our application example and (2) the mechanism we use to create decision models, i.e. models where we relate the created transformation rules to validate feature configurations and we define the required execution ordering of such transformation rules to derive configured products.

4.6.1. *Transformation rules in the Smart-Home systems SPL*

As we introduced before (see Figure 4.3 and Figure 4.13), the transformation rules we have created for our application example are used in four stages. The first set of rules is defined from the domain metamodel to the facilities metamodel. They are created taking into account the facilities feature model. The second set is defined from the facilities metamodel to the components metamodel. The third set is defined from the components metamodel to the architecture metamodel, taking into account the architecture feature model. Finally, the fourth set of transformation rules includes model-to-text transformations, which produce the source code of product line members.

First stage: Domain-to-facilities transformation rules. The purpose of these transformation rules is the adding of information about Smart-Homes' facilities to domain models. These are horizontal model-to-model transformations. It means, they transform models inside the same abstraction level, the application domain abstraction level, by adding concerns related to Smart-Homes' facilities.

In this stage, we create two sets of transformation rules: the *base* and the *specific* ones. On the one hand, base transformation rules do not depend on any variant of the product line. They are responsible for building the common or base product. Thus, they are always executed during the transformation process. For instance, we create a base transformation rule to transform `Domain metamodel::House` elements into `FacilitiesMetamodel::House` elements. Similarly, we create a base transformation rule to transform

`Domain metamodel::Floor` elements into `Facilities Metamodel::Floor` elements.

On the other hand, we create specific transformation rules taking into account the possible features that can affect the transformation process. In this case, those are features from the facilities feature model. For instance, we create two transformation rules to transform `Domain metamodel::Window` elements. The first one, taking into account the `Automatic Windows` feature, creates `FacilitiesMetamodel::Automatic (Window)` elements and one `FacilitiesMetamodel::WindowsController` element for each created `Room` element. The second one, taking into account the `Air Conditioning` feature, creates `FacilitiesMetamodel::Manual (Window)` elements and one `FacilitiesMetamodel::AirConditioning` element for each created `Room` element. Therefore, if the feature `Automatic Windows` is selected, the first transformation rule must be executed; if the feature `Air Conditioning` is selected, the second transformation rule must be executed.

Similarly, we create two different transformation rules to transform `Domain metamodel::Door` elements. The first one creates `FacilitiesMetamodel::Door` elements containing a `Domain metamodel::Fingerprint` element; the second one creates `FacilitiesMetamodel::Door` elements containing a `Domain metamodel::Keypad` element. The model-to-model and the model-to-text transformation rules we have created for our application example are available in the website [ARB].

Second stage: Facilities-to-components transformation rules. The second set of transformation rules is defined from the facilities metamodel to the components metamodel. These are vertical model-to-model transformations since they transform models between different abstraction levels. The source abstraction level is the application domain abstraction level, the target one is the abstraction level including concerns related to software components.

We create only base transformation rules given that there are no feature models affecting this transformation stage. However, in this particular case, not all the base transformation rules are always executed. Their execution depends on the transformation of the facility models. For instance, if at least one `FacilitiesMetamodel::WindowsController` element exists, then a base transformation rule in charge of creating a component that serves as controller for the automatic windows is executed.

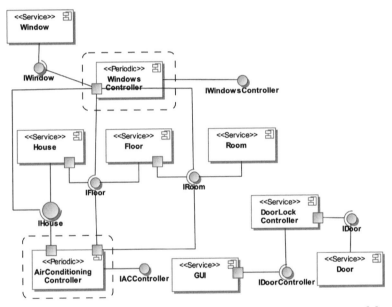

Figure 4.15. *Example of a Smart-Home systems' components model*

Figure 4.15 presents an example of a derived component model. This model is presented using the UML2 syntax. `Periodic` components in this model can either remain `Periodic` components after the next transformation stage, which creates architecture models, or not. The components inside dashed squares are not always created. The following conditions are required to create such components:

– The rule to create the `WindowController` component, its ports and interfaces, is only executed if there exists at least one `FacilitiesMetamodel::WindowsController` element in the source model.

– The rule to create the `AirConditioningController` component, its ports, and interfaces, is only executed if there exists at least one `Facilities Metamodel::AirConditioning` element in the source model.

The `GUI` component corresponds to the graphical user interface (GUI) of the Smart-Home systems. This component requires services of all the other components. In Figure 4.15, we only include one of its `Required` interfaces, `IDoorController`.

Third stage: Components-to-architecture transformation rules. The purpose of these transformation rules is the adding to component models information about the type of the components, *periodic* or *service*, and their instantiation mode, *on invocation* or *on deployment*. These are horizontal model-to-model transformations given that models are transformed inside the same abstraction level.

In this stage, we create base and specific transformation rules. For instance, we create a base transformation rule to transform `ComponentMetamodel::Interface` elements into `ArchitectureMetamodel::Interface` elements.

We create specific transformation rules taking into account the possible features that can affect the transformation process. In this case, those are features from the architecture feature model. For instance, we create two transformation rules to transform `ComponentMetamodel::Component` elements. The first one, taking into account the `Service` feature, creates `ArchitectureMetamodel::Service` (Component) elements. The second one, taking into account the `Periodic` feature, creates `ArchitectureMetamodel::Periodic` (Component) elements from `ComponentMetamodel::Periodic` elements. Therefore, if the feature `Service` is selected, the first transformation rule must be executed; if the feature `Periodic` is selected the second transformation rule must be executed.

Similarly, we create two different specific transformation rules to transform `Domain metamodel::Door` elements. The first one creates `FacilitiesMetamodel::Door` elements; each one containing a `Domain metamodel::Fingerprint` element; the second one creates `Facilities Metamodel::Door` elements; each one containing a `Domain metamodel::Keypad` element.

Fourth stage: Model-to-text transformation rules. The model-to-text transformation rules produce the source code of product line members. These transformation rules have as input an architecture model and a facilities model. On the one hand, the architecture model is transformed into the source code of OSGi components (Bundles) as presented in Figure 4.15. For this transformation, it is also possible to re-use pieces of code previously written by product line architects. Thus, the transformation rules are only in charge of connecting the already created pieces of code representing components.

On the other hand, the facilities model is transformed into an extra OSGi component, *HouseStructure*, which manages the structural design of the configured Smart-Home. Thus, if the Smart-Home has been configured to have one floor and two rooms, the *HouseStructure* component maintains this structure to provide the required services to the configured structural element. These model-to-text transformation rules are available along with the model-to-model transformation rules on the Website [ARB 12].

Figure 4.16 presents an example of the GUI corresponding to one configured Smart-Home System. The Smart-Home system was configured to have one floor with one room, the `Main Room`. This room has `Automatic Windows` as `Environmental Control`. The only door in the `Main Room` has `Fingerprint` as `Door Lock Control`.

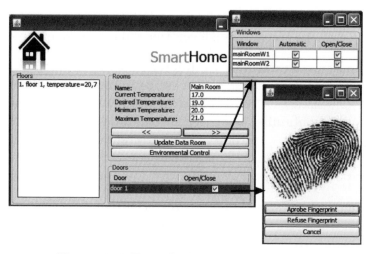

Figure 4.16. *Example of a Smart-Home system*

4.6.2. *Creating and using decision models*

In the previous section, we explained how we created specific transformation rules taking into account the possible features that can affect a model transformation stage. For instance, in the first transformation stage, those are features from the facilities feature model.

Remember one objective of an MD-SPL approach is to automate as far as possible the production plan. This "big process", thanks to MDE, can be viewed as an assembly of model transformations from requirements until code and tests. Thus, it implies defining a mechanism that enables selecting and executing automatically the base transformation rules and only some specific transformation rules. These are specific rules related to selected features in feature configurations. This mechanism must also ensure the correct execution ordering, also called execution scheduling, of the selected transformation rules. By correct, we mean an execution ordering that allows derivation of the required configured product.

We propose the use of explicit decision models in the context of MDE as a mechanism for composing transformation rules based on feature configurations [ARB 09]. This mechanism can be used in conjunction with transformation languages that provide facilities for the composition of transformation rules. In particular, we used the oAW modeling framework and the Xtend and Xpand model transformation languages, which provide a mechanism based on Aspect-Oriented Programming (AOP) for composing transformation rules (see section 3.6.4).

Our decision models are useful to capture (1) the relationships between features and specific transformation rules, and (2) the required execution ordering of transformation rules to create products based on feature configurations. Our basic idea to obtain a final execution scheduling is to construct a baseline ordering, modified according to valid feature configurations. A baseline ordering describes a sequence of calls to base transformation rules. Our mechanism to adapt the baseline ordering is supported by AOP concepts. We capture in decision models information about *aspects* that must be woven with a baseline ordering to adapt it. Aspects maintain the information of what base transformation rules must be intercepted (join points) and what specific transformation rules must then be executed (advices) according to defined *conditions* on feature configurations.

Table 4.1 presents examples of conditions on feature configurations that we can capture in our decision models. These conditions imply modifying a baseline ordering. In the first column, we present examples of conditions; in the second column, we present the name of the base rule in the baseline ordering to be intercepted (join point); in the third column, we present the name of the specific rule (advice) to be executed if the condition appears in a feature configuration. Thus, if the Feature One appears Selected in a feature configuration, regardless of the other features, Rule A must be intercepted and the Rule A' must be executed instead. If Feature Two appears Unselected in a feature configuration, regardless of the other features, the `Rule B` must be intercepted and the `Rule B'` must be executed instead. We can also capture more complex conditions. For instance, in row three, we express that if the `Feature One` appears `Unselected` and the `Feature Three` appears `Selected` in a feature configuration, regardless of the other features, the `Rule A` must be intercepted and the `Rule C` must be executed instead.

Condition	Join point	Advice
Feature One Selected	Rule A	Rule A'
Feature Two Unselected	Rule B	Rule B'
Feature One Unselected and Feature Three Selected	Rule A	Rule C

Table 4.1. *Examples of conditions on feature configurations that imply an adaptation of a baseline (transformation rules') ordering*

For example, in the context of our smart home application, during the derivation of a Smart-Home system, if the feature `Automatic Windows` is selected in a feature configuration, the base sequence to transform domain models into facilities models must be modified. This modification is done in a defined point to include an alternative step where the transformation rule in charge of creating automatic windows is called. Figure 4.17 presents a small part of our decision model to transform domain models into facilities models. Firstly, we define a baseline ordering including the execution of the transformation rules `domainFloorsToFacilitiesFloors` and `domain WindowsToFacilitiesWindows`. Secondly, we create an aspect indicating that if the feature `Automatic Windows` is selected in a feature configuration, the execution of the base transformation rule `domainWindowsToFacilitiesWindows` must be intercepted and the specific transformation rule `windowsToAutomaticWindows` must then be executed.

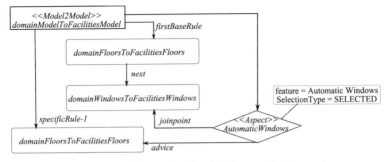

Figure 4.17. *Example of a decision model to create Smart-Home systems*

Our decision models also allows us to capture the different transformation stages included in a product line derivation process. For our application example, these are four transformation stages, from domain models to obtaining Java source code. This type of composition, which composes transformation rules using the output model of a rule as the input model of another rule is called external composition [WAG 08a]. Figure 4.18 presents the part of our decision model capturing the external composition required for deriving Smart-Home systems given our four transformation stages. We create this model using the decision model editor which we will present in Chapter 6. In section 5.4, we discuss limitations of our mechanism to derive products based on decision models.

The decision metamodel. Figure 4.19 presents the decision metamodel we have created to create decision models. A model transformation `Workflow` contains a sequence of `TransformationPrograms`. A `TransformationProgram` is either a `Model2Model` or a `Model2Text` transformation. Each `TransformationProgram` uses a set of `Transformation Rules` and a set of `Aspects` to perform its process of transformation. As introduced before, we classify `TransformationRules` in `Base` and `Specific` ones. An `Aspect` specifies its `advice`, which is a `Specific` transformation rule, and its join point, which in turn is a `Base` transformation rule. A `Workflow` must take into account a set of `ExecutionConditions`, which depends on a set of `Features` with a particular `SelectionType`, `SELECTED` or `NOT_ SELECTED`. Finally, an `Aspect` must be woven if its `executionCondition` appears in a feature configuration.

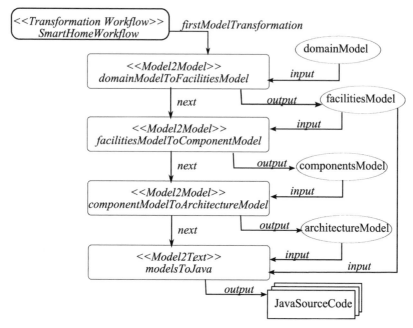

Figure 4.18. *Decision model including external composition*

Creating executable model transformation workflows from decision models. As we mentioned before, we use the oAW modeling framework and the Xtend and Xpand model transformation languages to implement our approach and application example. We then transformed our decision models into oAW workflows that include the required instructions (1) to execute model transformations in different stages (external composition), and (2) to modify a baseline ordering of a set of transformation rules (internal composition [WAG 08a]). For transforming our decision models into oAW workflows, we created a model-to-text transformation. This model-to-text transformation is provided at [ARB 12]. We use it in the decision models editor (Chapter 6) to provide the facility of transforming decision models into executable oAW workflows.

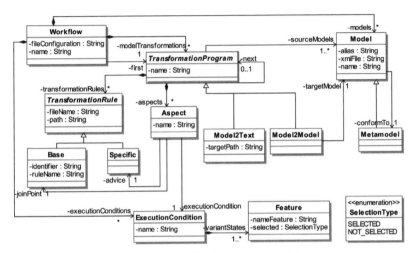

Figure 4.19. *Decision metamodel*

Listing 4.1 presents a part of a sample generated oAW workflow. This workflow specifies that the transformation rule `domainWindowsToFacilitiesWindows` is intercepted (line 2-3 and line 9) and the transformation rule `adviceWindowsToAutomaticWindows` is executed (line 5) if the feature `Automatic Windows` is selected in a feature configuration (line 1).

```
1  <Feature selected="Automatic_Windows">
2    <transformationAspect adviceTarget=
3                    "domainWindowsToFacilitiesWindows">
4      <extensionAdvice
5        value="adviceWindowsToAutomaticWindows" />
6    </transformationAspect>
7  </Feature>
8
9  <transform id="domainWindowsToFacilitiesWindows">
10   <invoke value="domainWindowsToFacilitiesWindows" />
11 </transform>
```

Listing 4.1. *Example of an oAW workflow*

4.7. Summary

Software product line engineering brings benefits in terms of costs and productivity by taking advantage of the commonality. Model driven engineering techniques and tools have, without any doubt, the potential to significantly increase the productivity and quality of software engineering processes. Although the integration of both approaches is promising, it requires a tight coupling and tuning of the derivation chain. This chapter exposes a general view of the MDE product line and some issues about capturing the variability of different software views and configuring and deriving products in a multi-staged process. The notion of view has been used for years in software engineering. It is mandatory to develop complex systems with several stakeholders: requirement analysts, architects, designers, programmers, concerned with several different aspects of the software system (requirements, architectures, GUI, persistence, concurrency, distribution, etc.).

This chapter focuses on capturing the variability in different models conforming to metamodels, configuring the product, and defining an automated production chain relying on a multi-staged process. We make explicit examples of variability models with the facilities and architectural feature models and we show how these models are taken into account in the transformation process. The derivation process is a complex task and it requires sequences of transformations that need a precise scheduling. Decision models are artifacts specifying base and specific transformation rules for scheduling the rules for both commonality and variability. To schedule these rules correctly, the mechanism uses aspect-oriented programming. Decision models capture transformational aspects of the baseline derivation process to derive specific variable applications. This general MD-SPL process is effective but it is not always sufficiently flexible for fine-grained configuration. We need rather to configure differently several instances of the same kind of artifacts. The next chapter discusses this issue and presents the FieSta solution.

Chapter 5

The FieSta Framework: Fine-grained Derivation and Configuration

5.1. Introduction

In Chapter 4, we presented how MDE can be used to enhance SPLE. We have shown that models and model transformations can be used to support the configuration and derivation of product line members, respectively. We have also noted that these MD-SPL approaches are not enough to configure and derive products with fine-grained variations. These approaches have some limitations to express variability and to configure products, and they do not provide appropriate mechanisms to derive products that facilitate the maintenance, re-use, and evolution of core assets such as transformation rules. This chapter first introduces the concepts of coarse-grained and fine-grained variations. Our solution to fix this issue is called FieSta, for *Fine-grained derivation and configuration for Software product lines*. This approach relies on constraint and binding models, which are described and illustrated. We present our proposal to improve the expressive power of variability in section 5.2; we introduce a mechanism to capture and express *fine-grained variations* between products of an MD-SPL. Finally, we present our mechanisms for deriving configured products supported by decision models in section 5.3. At the end of this chapter, we present limitations of FieSta in section 5.4.

5.1.1. *Coarse-grained and fine-grained variations*

The base mechanisms which we have introduced until now in this book allow product line architects to capture and express the possible variations between members of a product line by separately creating metamodels and feature models. This allows us to capture and express *coarse-grained variations* between products. For example, a Smart-Home system has a coarse-grained variation, with respect to the `Automatic Windows` feature, if either all or none of the `Windows` in the Smart-Home products generated from the product line are `Automatic Windows`. Rephrasing it, a coarse-grained feature may be selected for all the models conforming to a given concept. Thus, a coarse-grained variation applies uniformly to all the instances of a metaconcept.

We obtain coarse-grained variations between members of our product line example by creating coarse-grained configurations. A *coarse-grained configuration* is an association between models that conform to metamodels and instances of feature models. Thus, for instance, a first Smart-Home system can be coarse-grained configured by creating a domain model and selecting the feature `Fingerprint`. A second Smart-Home system can be coarse-grained configured by using the same domain model and selecting the feature `Keypad`. When Smart-Home systems are derived, a coarse-grained variation between them appears: all the `Doors` in the first Smart-Home system have `Fingerprint` as lock door control mechanism, and all the `Doors` in the second Smart-Home system have `Keypad` as lock door control mechanism. One immediate solution to this problem is to refine the model and to introduce more specific models making some of the variations explicit. If the degree of variation is not high, this is a good solution; but in many real situations, this is not acceptable. Thus, we need to introduce concepts and constructs to solve this issue.

We propose to improve the expressive power of variability by providing a mechanism we have named *fine-grained variations* between products of an MD-SPL. For instance, the first Smart-Home system can have a fine-grained variation in relation to the second Smart-Home system if both systems have automatic windows, but they may differ in the specific windows that are automatic. Additionally, we propose a mechanism to create *fine-grained configurations*, which allows us to configure model elements individually based on features. For example, by creating a fine-grained configuration, we could configure the `mainRoom` to manage `Air Conditioning` as environmental control and the `livingRoom` to manage `Automatic Windows` as environmental control [ARB 09]. A coarse-grained variation can be viewed as a "class variation" conversely, a fine-grained variation is an "instance variation" that is specific to one instance of a concept. The product line architect has to analyze the domain variability, to choose between coarse-grained and fine-grained variations accordingly with its structural metamodel.

To solve the problem of fine-grained configuration, one can define metaconcepts associated with every relevant combination of features and structural elements. For instance, we can have a metaconcept of `RoomWithAutomaticWindow` and `RoomWithManualWindow`. However, this is not a scalable approach and we propose a more definitive solution. The solution is to define links between features and particular elements of the structural model. However, we should continue to propose coarse-grained variation in a context where group features and cardinality are possible. Thus, we need to add some constraints to avoid illegal configurations and a mechanism to check the configuration validity.

5.2. Binding models and constraint models

The mechanisms we propose are based on what we have named *constraint models* and *binding models*. To facilitate the understanding of our proposal, first we introduce our mechanism for configuring products by using binding models. Afterwards, we present our approach to improve the expressive power of variability in MD-SPLs by using constraint models.

5.2.1. *Binding models*

We call the relationship between a model element and a feature a *binding*. For example, let us assume that the livingRoom (see Figure 4.5) has Air Conditioning as environmental control mechanism (see Figure 4.11). A binding B is a pair $B = [E, F]$ composed of a model element E and a feature F, where F is either a SolitaryFeature or a GroupedFeature. For example, a product designer can create a binding relating the livingRoom and the Automatic Windows feature, $B = [$livingRoom, Automatic Windows$]$.

DEFINITION 5.1.– *We define a* binding model *as the set of bindings defined by a product designer between a model that conforms to a metamodel and a feature model, which conforms to a feature metamodel.*

Figure 5.1 presents a binding model example for our case study. This binding model is created between the domain model from Figure 4.5 and the facilities feature model from Figure 4.11. binding1 configures the livingRoomD1 to have Keypad as Lock Door Control. binding2 denotes the designer selection of Air Conditioning in the livingRoom as environmental control system. Finally, binding3 defines that the mainRoomW1 is configured to be an Automatic Window. Chapter 6 will present tools to help in binding and configuring products in FieSta; it also gives an example of the configuration and derivation of a Smart-Home system of our case study. The example includes a binding model between a component model and the architecture feature model.

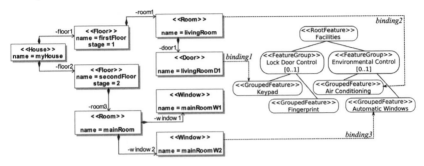

Figure 5.1. *Binding model example*

5.2.2. *Constraint models*

Product line architects must use *constraint models* to restrict the bindings between model elements and features; for example, to express that only domain models can be bound to facilities models, or that maximum three Room elements can be bound to the feature Air Conditioning.

A constraint model is a set of *constraints*.

DEFINITION 5.2. – *A constraint is a quadruple* $C = [M, F, A, D]$ *composed of a metaconcept M, a feature F, and two properties: A and D. A constraint C expresses the fact that model elements that conform to the metaconcept M can be bound to the feature F.*

The properties A and D are described in sections 5.2.3 and 5.2.4. Each constraint is unique in a constraint model; this means, only one constraint includes a pair $[M, F]$. Our constraints serve to avoid inconsistencies during the configuration and derivation processes. Constraints must prevent the following problems:

– Any model is bound to any feature model. For example, in our case study, only domain models can be bound to the facilities feature models and only components models can be bound to the architecture feature models.

– Model elements that conform to any metaconcept are bound to any feature. For example, for a requirement of the product line (R1) specifying that only windows can be automatic, a constraint must exclude Door elements from the Automatic Windows feature.

– Any number of model elements that conform to a metaconcept is bound to any number of features. For example, since the installation of automatic windows could be expensive in a product line for economical Smart-Homes, a product line architect may deal with a requirement (R2) that specifies that only (maximum) one window can be automatic. Thus, a constraint must prevent more than one Window element from being bound to the Automatic Windows feature.

– Model elements and features are bound without taking into account constraints between functional requirements. For example, for a requirement of the product line (R3), which specifies that automatic windows must have sensors, a constraint must prevent Window elements without an associated Sensor element from being configured as Automatic Windows.

– Model elements and features are bound without taking into account the prerequisites of the configuration. For example, a requirement of the product line (R4) specifies that automatic windows can only be selected from rooms, which are not configured to have air conditioning. A constraint must prevent Window elements with their rooms associated to the Air Conditioning feature being configured as Automatic Windows.

Therefore, for our case study, with respect to the requirement (R1), a product line architect could define a constraint between the Window metaconcept and the Automatic Windows feature, constraint1=[Window, Automatic Windows, A, D]. The constraint describes that during the configuration of a product, product designers can bind Window elements; for example, the mainRoomW2 with the feature Automatic Windows (see Figure 5.1). Another constraint can be created between the Door metaconcept and the Lock Door Control feature, constraint2=[Door, Lock Door Control, A, D]. The constraint describes that product designers can bind Door elements with either the feature Keypad or the feature Fingerprint. Figure 5.2 presents these constraints. In Chapter 6, we present the constraint models we created for the SPL of our Smart-Home system.

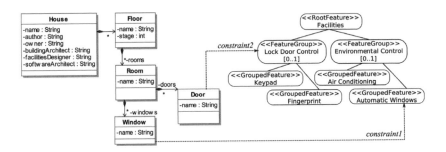

Figure 5.2. *Constraint model example*

A product line architect could also define a constraint between the Room metaconcept and the Automatic Windows feature, like in constraint3 for R3. The constraint describes that product designers may bind Room elements with the feature Automatic Windows to indicate that all the windows in the bound room are automatic windows. Product line architects can add descriptions to constraints to help product designers during the creation of bindings. Thus, for constraint1 we added the description: "A window may be an automatic window"; for constraint3: "All the windows in a room may be automatic windows".

5.2.3. *The cardinality property*

To fulfill the requirement $R2$ presented before, which specifies that only (maximum) one window can be automatic, our approach includes the definition of the cardinality property (A). The cardinality property is similar in form to feature cardinality.

DEFINITION 5.3.– *We define cardinality as a UML-like cardinality $A = [i..j]$, where $i <= j$, i and j are natural numbers, and j can be denoted by $*$ to express an unbounded number. Cardinality (A) adds semantics to a constraint $C = [M, F, A, D]$ by expressing the fact that the designer can create a restricted number of bindings between model elements that conform to M and the feature F (a number between i and j).*

The requirement ($R2$) is an example where cardinality is required to limit the number of bindings among model elements and features. This indicates that only (a maximum) one window can be automatic.

The next two subsections present the semantics of the cardinality property in a constraint. The semantics depend on the type of feature included in the constraint, i.e. group, grouped or solitary. The introduction of the cardinality property specifies the cardinality of the original features in the feature model.

Cardinality on Solitary and Grouped Features. In a constraint $C = [M, F, A = [i..j], D]$ where F is a solitary or grouped feature, the meanings of i and j are respectively the minimum and maximum number of model elements that conform to M that can be bound to F. For example, if a product line architect wants to restrict to 0 or 1 the number of automatic windows, he must add the cardinality $A = [0..1]$ to the `constraint1` presented in Figure 5.2. Thus, maximum one window could be automatic, e.g. the `mainRoomW2` (see Figure 5.1).

Cardinality on Group Features. In a constraint $C = [M, F, A = [i..j], D]$ where F is a group feature, the meanings of i and j are respectively the minimum and maximum number of features grouped by F that can be bound to a particular model element that conforms to M.

For example, for a requirement of the product line specifying that lock doors control can be managed by using either keypad or fingerprint, the product line architect creates a constraint using the Room metaconcept and the Lock Door Control feature, constraint2= [Door, Lock Door Control, A, D] (see Figure 5.2). The architect sets the cardinality $A = [0..1]$, constraining to zero or one the number of grouped features (Fingerprint, Keypad) that can be bound to a Door element. Thus a door, e.g. the livingRoomD1 (Figure 5.1), can be bound to only one of the features Keypad or Fingerprint.

When a group feature F has the cardinality $[n..m]$, the cardinality of a constraint $C = [M, F, A, D]$ has to be inside the limits of the cardinality of F. It implies that if the cardinality $A = [i..j]$ then $n \leq i \leq j \leq m$. This ensures that constraint models are consistent with feature models used for their construction.

5.2.4. *The structural dependency property*

DEFINITION 5.4. – *The structural dependency property D in a $C = [M, F, A, D]$, denotes conditions that model elements have to satisfy to be bound to specific features.*

An example from requirement $R3$ presented before is that automatic windows must have sensors. In this case, the model elements we identified in the conditions are Window and Sensor, and the feature is Automatic Windows. Thus, to bind a Window element to the Automatic Windows feature, allowed by the constraint1, the Window element should have a Sensor element.

Another example is a requirement specifying that only one room can have automatic windows. This requirement defines the requirement ($R1$), specifying that windows must be localized in the same room. Then, only `Window` elements from the same `Room` element can be bound to the `Automatic Windows` feature.

We also use the structural dependency property to describe dependencies between bindings. For example, the requirement ($R4$), which specifies that only automatic windows can be selected from rooms that are not configured to have air conditioning, implies that a `Window` element can be bound to the `Automatic Windows` feature only if the `Room` element where the window is located is not bound to the `Air Conditioning` feature.

We express the value of the property D as a set of OCL sentences (see section 3.3). For example, for the requirement ($R3$) a product line architect must set the structural dependency property of the `constraint1` to $D = \{$`sensor->notEmpty()`$\}$.

5.2.5. *The constraint metamodel and the binding metamodel*

Constraint and binding models have their own metamodel, which is described in this section.

5.2.5.1. *The constraint metamodel*

We have created a *constraint metamodel* to facilitate the creation of constraint models. Our constraint metamodel is based on our feature metamodel (see Figure 4.10). We extended its semantics to include the constraints for managing binding models.

Figure 5.3 presents our constraint metamodel. The main new concepts and attributes added to our feature metamodel are the following:

– GroupConstraint. It allows us to create constraints including group features;

– Constraint. It allows us to create constraints including solitary or grouped features;

– fineMin and fineMax attributes. They allow us to relate the cardinality property to constraints;

– OCLExpression. It represents the structural dependency property of constraints;

– Metaconcept. It represents metaconcepts related to constraints.

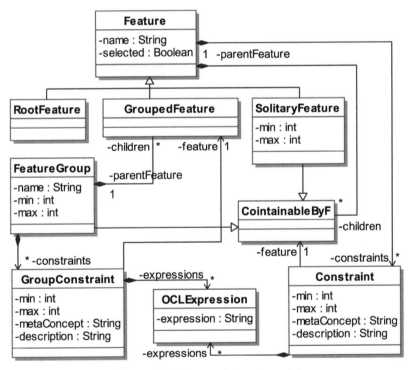

Figure 5.3. *Constraint metamodel*

Thus, in a constraint $C = [M, F, A, D]$, C conforms either to `GroupConstraint` or `Constraint`, M conforms to `MetaConcept`; F conforms to either `Grouped` or `CointainableByF` (`Group` or `Solitary`), i and j (from $A = [i, j]$) conforms to `fineMin` and `fineMax`, and D conforms to `OCLExpression`.

5.2.5.2. *The binding metamodel*

To introduce the concept of binding, we create a *binding metamodel*, Figure 5.4. This metamodel extends our constraint metamodel with concepts for binding model elements to features. Thus, a set of `Configurations` associated with a `RootFeature` can be created. A `Configuration` groups a set of bindings between `Features` and model elements. We maintain the information of model elements as properties of the `Binding` metaconcept, `metaconceptName`, and `elementName`.

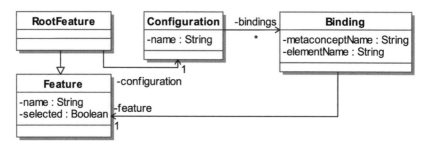

Figure 5.4. *Binding metamodel*

5.2.6. *Validating binding models against constraint models*

We say a binding $B = [E, F_1]$ *satisfies* a constraint $C = [M, F_2, A, D]$ when E conforms to M, $F_1 = F_2$, and B satisfies the restrictions defined by the properties A and D. We note this relationship $B \overset{s}{\rightarrow} C$. For example, `binding3` from Figure 5.1 satisfies the `constraint1` from Figure 5.2 because `mainRoomW2` conforms to `Window` and B satisfies the restrictions defined by the properties A and D of the constraint1. The validation of a binding model against a constraint model implies that every existing binding *satisfies* one constraint in the constraint model.

We validate existing bindings in a binding model automatically against a set of OCL-type sentences that we generate from each constraint in a constraint model. For example, if the feature involved in the constraint $C = [\$metaConcept, \$feature, [\$fineMin, \$fineMax], D]$ is a grouped or solitary feature, we generate the sentence in Listing 5.1. The dollar symbol $ denotes variables and the operator aCollection->between(a,b) is equivalent to the expression (aCollection->size()$\geq$a) && (aCollection->size()$\leq$b). Listing 5.2 presents the particular sentence generated for the constraint= [Window, Automatic Windows, [0..1], D], where D = bindings-> select(b|b.elementName=="mainRoomW1")-> between(0,0). In this case, D specifies that there cannot exist any binding where the mainRoomW1 is involved.

```
1
2 Context Configuration inv:
3 bindings->select(b|b.feature.name=$feature and
4    b.metaConceptName=$metaConcept)->between($fineMin,fineMax$) and $D$;
```

Listing 5.1. *Example of a generated OCL-type sentence*

```
1
2 Context Configuration inv:
3 bindings->select(b|b.feature.name="Automatic_Windows"
4    and b.metaConceptName="Window")->between(0,1)
5    and bindings->select(b|b.elementName="mainRoomW1")->between(0,0);
```

Listing 5.2. *Example of a generated OCL-type sentence*

For the generation of OCL sentences, we have created model-to-text transformation rules. These transformation rules generate *Check* expressions. Check is a language included in the oAW framework which allows us to validate models against OCL-type expressions [OAW 09]. We generate Check expressions from the constraint models we create using the constraint models creator that we later present in Chapter 6. Therefore, product designers are able to validate binding models against the generated Check expressions. We include details of the model-to-text transformation rules in charge of creating Check expression on the Website [ARB]. In Chapter 6 we present a complete example of the staged configuration and derivation of Smart-Home systems of our MD-SPL. This example includes examples of the generated Check expressions for our constraint models.

5.3. Deriving products based on constraint models and binding models

In section 4.6.2, we introduced decision models in the context of MDE as our mechanism for composition of transformation rules based on feature configurations. We discussed how our decision models are useful to capture (1) the relationships between features and specific transformation rules, and (2) the required execution ordering of transformation rules to create products based on feature configurations.

Our basic idea of obtaining a final execution scheduling was to construct a baseline scheduling, which is modified according to valid feature configurations. Thus, for example, during the derivation of a Smart-Home system, if the feature `Automatic Windows` was selected in a feature configuration, the base sequence to transform domain models into facilities models was modified to replace the rule `domainWindowsToFacilitiesWindows` by the rule `windowsToAutomaticWindows`.

Binding models imply the modification of a baseline scheduling taking into account not only features from feature configurations, but also bindings from binding models. Thus, for example, if any `Window` element is bound to the feature `Automatic Windows` in a binding model, the base sequence to transform domain models into facilities models must be modified. This modification implies replacing the rule `domainWindowsToFacilitiesWindows` by the rule `particularWindowsToAutomaticWindows`. This rule must transform only the `Domain metamodel::Window` elements, which are bound to the `Automatic Windows` feature, into `FacilitiesMetamodel:Automatic` window elements. For instance, from the binding model presented in Figure 5.1, given that the `mainRoomW2` is the only window bound to the feature `Automatic Windows`, this is the only window that must be transformed into an automatic window.

Condition	Join point	Advice
Exists at least one binding $B_1 = [E_1, F_1]$ that satisfies the constraint $C_1 = [M_1, F_1, A, D]$	Rule A	Rule A'(E_1)
Feature Two Unselected and exists at least one binding $B_2 = [E_2, F_2]$ that satisfies the constraint $C_2 = [M_2, F_2, A, D]$	Rule B	Rule B'(E_2)

Table 5.1. *Examples of fine-grained conditions on feature configurations which imply to adapt a baseline (transformation rules') scheduling*

Table 5.1 presents examples of conditions on binding models that we can capture in our extended decision models. These conditions imply the modification of a baseline scheduling. In the first column, we present examples of conditions; in the second column, we present the name of the base rule in the baseline scheduling to be intercepted (join point); in the third column, we present the name of the specific rule (advice) to be executed if the condition appears in a binding model. We express conditions in terms of bindings that satisfy constraints. Thus, row one in Table 5.1 expresses that if at least one binding $B_1 = [E_1, F_1]$ that satisfies the constraint $C_1 = [M_1, F_1, A, D]$ in a binding model exists, `Rule A` must be intercepted and `Rule A'` must be executed instead using E_1 as a parameter. We can also capture conditions, which have taken into account not only bindings, but also a selection of features. For instance, in row two, we express that if `Feature Two` appears `Unselected` and at least one binding $B_2 = [E_2, F_2]$ exists that satisfies the constraint $C_2 = [M_2, F_2, A, D]$ in a binding model, `Rule B` must be intercepted and `Rule B'` must be executed instead using E_2 as parameter.

Figure 5.5 presents a small part of our decision model to transform domain models into facilities models by taking into account binding models. Similarly, as presented before in section 4.6.2, we first define a baseline scheduling, which includes the execution of the transformation rules `domainFloorsToFacilitiesFloors` and `domain WindowsToFacilitiesWindows`. Then, we create an aspect indicating that if some bindings satisfies the `constraint1` (which describes that product designers can bind `Window` elements with the feature `Automatic Windows`) the execution of the base transformation rule `domain WindowsToFacilitiesWindows` must be intercepted. After the interception is done, the specific transformation rule `particularWindowsToAutomatic Windows` must be then executed. This rule queries the binding model used to configure the product that is derived and transforms only the `Window`

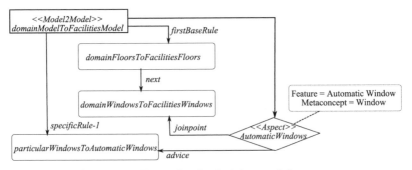

Figure 5.5. *Example of a decision model to create Smart-Home systems with binding models*

elements bound to the `Automatic Windows` feature. In section 5.4, we discuss some limitations of our mechanism to derive products based on decision models.

5.3.1. *The extended decision metamodel*

We extended the decision metamodel that we presented before in Figure 4.19. Figure 5.6 presents our extended decision metamodel, which allows us to derive products taking into account binding models.

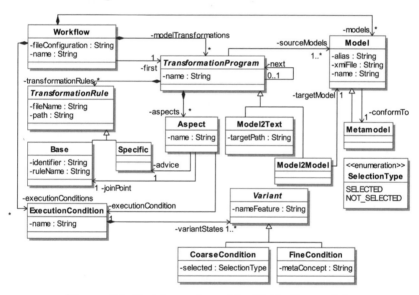

Figure 5.6. *Decision metamodel with binding models*

We still include the concepts of `Workflow`, `TransformationProgram`, `Transformationrule`, and `Aspect`. We modify, however, the concept of `Execution Condition`. In this extended decision, metamodel an `ExecutionCondition`, depends on a set of `Variants`, which we specialized in `CoarseCondition` and `FineCondition`. A `CoarseCondition` represents a feature that can be `SELECTED`/`NOT_SELECTED`. A `FineCondition` represents a constraint.

Thus, based on a binding model, we can indicate that a Specific transformation rule must be woven with a Base transformation rule when bindings that satisfy the constraint denoted by a FineCondition element exist. For instance, we can indicate that a specific transformation rule must be woven with a base transformation rule when the feature Air Conditioning appears bound to a Window element.

5.3.2. *Creating executable model transformation workflows from decision models and constraint models*

As presented earlier, we transform our decision models into oAW workflows, which include the required instructions to execute model transformations in different stages (external composition), and modify a baseline scheduling of a set of transformation rules (internal composition). For transforming our decision models into oAW workflows taking into account constraint models and binding models, we modified the model-to-text transformation we introduced before in section 4.6.2. This model-to-text transformation allows us to generate executable oAW from decision models. The oAW generated script contains a querying mechanism, which looks for bindings that satisfy particular constraints. Listing 5.3 presents a part of a generated oAW workflow. This workflow specifies that the transformation rule domainWindowsToFacilitiesWindows is intercepted (line 2-3 and line 9) and the transformation rule particular WindowsToAutomaticWindows is executed (line 4-5) if bindings that satisfy the constraint created between the Automatic Windows feature and the Window metaconcept (line 1) exist. We created the oAW component, which allows us to query binding models looking for bindings that satisfy a particular constraint. The line 1 from Listing 5.3 shows a call to our oAW component. The component queries a binding model, which has been previously loaded in the execution context of an oAW workflow. The model-to-text transformation we created to generate oAW workflows from decision models is available at [ARB 12].

```
1  <fineFeature toFeature="Automatic" boundMetaconcept="Window">
2    <transformationAspect
3      adviceTarget="domainWindowsToFacilitiesWindows">
4      <extensionAdvice
5        value="particularWindowsToAutomaticWindows" />
6    </transformationAspect>
7  </fineFeature>
8
9  <transform id="domainWindowsToFacilitiesWindows">
10   <invoke value="domainWindowsToFacilitiesWindows" />
11 </transform>
```

Listing 5.3. *Example of a generated oAW workflow*

5.4. Identified limitations

In previous sections, we discussed how our decision models are useful to capture the relationships between features and/or bindings, and specific transformation rules, and how the required execution scheduling of transformation rules to create products is based on feature configurations and/or binding models. Our idea to obtain a final execution scheduling was to construct a baseline scheduling, which is modified according to execution conditions defined in terms of feature configurations and/or binding models. We have identified at least three limitations in our strategy of relating execution conditions to specific transformation rules. Two of them occur when conditions only take into account feature configurations (see Table 4.1). The other one occurs when conditions take into account not only feature configurations, but also binding models (see Table 5.1).

5.4.1. *Features combinatorial*

The first limitation of our approach is that the number of valid feature configurations, which can be created based on one feature model could be high. In our current approach, we do not include mechanisms to guarantee that either for all possible valid feature configurations there is a set of transformation rules in charge of generating a runnable product, or that in our decision models we include execution conditions that take into account each valid feature configuration. Currently, this is the responsibility of the product line architects.

We have made some attempts to manipulate feature models in SPLE using the concurrent constraint programming (CCP) paradigm in [ARB 10]. The novelty of our approach is that we facilitate the management of feature interactions to architects.

5.4.2. *Features interaction*

A feature interaction occurs when a feature modifies or influences another feature in defining the overall system behavior [CAL 03]. Generally, such an interaction occurs when two items have some intersections and their execution does not commute. For example, assume a feature model including three features, A, B, and C. If the feature A interacts with the features B and C, the selection in a feature configuration of A and B will imply baseline scheduling. The selection of A and C will imply a different adaptation and then the selection of the three would not produce the expected result. The problem of dealing with feature interactions is an important problem, which currently deserves special attention in the field of feature modeling [REI 09]. In our current approach, we take into account that the presence of one particular feature in different valid feature configurations may imply different adaptations of a baseline scheduling of transformation rules. For instance, in Table 4.1 the presence of the Feature One in two different possible feature configurations implies a different adaptation. In row one, we specify that if the Feature One appears Selected in a feature configuration, irrespective of the other features, Rule A must be intercepted and the Rule A' must be executed instead. In row three, we express that if Feature One appears Unselected and Feature Three appears Selected in a feature configuration, irrespective of the other features, `Rule A` must be intercepted and `Rule C` must be executed instead. Nevertheless, it is the responsibility of the product line architects (1) to identify feature interactions, (2) to define transformation rules for the different scenarios derived from feature interactions, (3) to define execution conditions for such scenarios and (4) to create and relate transformation rules to the defined execution conditions. Our approach does not provide mechanisms to validate that all possible feature interactions are taken into account.

5.4.3. *Bindings interaction*

When conditions take into account binding models (see Table 5.1), our approach allows product line architects to create decision models where decisions consider bindings satisfying only one constraint. For instance, row one in Table 5.1 expresses that if there exists at least one binding $B_1 = [E_1, F_1]$ that satisfies the constraint $C_1 = [M_1, F_1, A, D]$ in a binding model, `Rule A` must be intercepted and `Rule A'` must be executed instead using E_1 as parameter. In this case, we only consider bindings satisfying one constraint, C_1. To understand why we cannot consider bindings that satisfy more than one constraint, let us assume the following scenario. Suppose we have a condition expressing that if there exists in a binding model at least one binding $B_1 = [E_1, F_1]$ that satisfies the constraint $C_1 = [M_1, F_1, A, D]$ and at least one binding $B_2 = [E_2, F_2]$ that satisfies the constraint $C_2 = [M_2, F_2, A, D]$, then `Rule B` must be intercepted and `Rule B'` must be executed instead using E_1 and E_2 as parameter. Now, suppose we have a binding model with two bindings that satisfy C_1, $B_1 = [E_1, F_1]$ and $B_{1'} = [E_{1'}, F_1]$, and two bindings that satisfy C_2, $B_2 = [E_2, F_2]$ and $B_{2'} = [E_{2'}, F_2]$. In this case, it is not possible to know the ordering of the parameters to execute the `Rule B'`. It means, we are not able to know if we must invoke `Rule B'` (E_1, E_2), `Rule B'` $(E_{1'}, E_2)$, or `Rule B'` $(E_1, E_{2'})$. Therefore, if for each condition, we consider bindings satisfying several constraints, we cannot guarantee that the specific rules (advices) will be executed with the suitable parameters.

5.5. Summary

In this chapter, we first introduced the concept and the need for fine-grained variation and configuration. Fine-grained variation arises when we need to define variable artifacts of the same kind. Coarse-grained approaches do not allow us to configure differently the instances of the same metamodel. Introducing new models making some variations explicit could be possible, but it is not a general solution. To solve this issue, we introduce binding and constraint models. On the one hand, binding models allow us to capture the links between a model and a variability model, thus enabling the fine-grained configuration of model elements. On the other hand, the constraint model specifies precisely the semantics of the bindings using cardinality and structural dependency properties. This specification is based mainly on OCL sentences, which are common and supported by various validation tools. We have also described the metamodels we created to support the creation of constraint, binding, and decision models. Our basic idea to obtain a final execution scheduling was to construct a baseline scheduling, which is modified according to valid feature configurations. We tune our general strategy for validating binding models against constraint models and for generating executable model transformation workflows from decision models. Binding models imply modification of the baseline scheduling taking into account not only features from feature configurations, but also bindings from binding models. Aspects responsible for the rules scheduling associated with variations, query the binding model to get the precise element impacted by the rule. The decision metamodel has been extended to allow for the derivation of products taking into account binding models. Finally, we presented the limitations of our approach for deriving products based on decision models.

Chapter 6

Tools Support

6.1. Introduction

This chapter presents the use of FieSta, our MD-SPL approach, its tooling, and its application in the Smart-Home case study. We also present our implementation strategy for FieSta. The implementation strategy defines the general process for the implementation of our MD-SPL engineering mechanisms for creating product lines. Our implementation strategy includes the required activities to create products, and the tools we have created to support these activities. We present the tool support for expressing variability and configuring products in section 6.4, and the tool support for deriving configured products in section 6.5.

Our tool support assists product line architects and product designers during the whole development lifecycle of MD-SPLs. We provide Eclipse plug-ins to create MD-SPL projects, feature models, constraint models, binding models, OCL-type expressions to validate binding models against constraint models, and decision models. We also provide oAW components to facilitate the processing of binding models and decision models to derive products. For the implementation of our tool support, we chose EMF as the modeling framework, which means we express all our metamodels based on the Ecore meta-metamodel (see section 3.5.1). We opted to use oAW as our model transformation engine. We selected oAW because, as presented before in section 3.6.3, this is a complete MDE framework integrated with Eclipse that makes the reading, instantiation, checking, and transformation of models possible. oAW has been used successfully to create SPLs, and there is an active community of SPL and MDE developers using and improving it.

The entire FieSta toolkit, the instructions for installing it, and the two case studies can be found on the Website [ARB].

6.2. The FieSta process

The UML activity diagram in Figure 6.1 presents the general overview of the software process for FieSta. *Domain engineering* and *application engineering* organize the activities. For domain engineering, we built tools to support product line architects in the creation of a special type of Eclipse project, MD-SPL project. An MD-SPL project includes the required oAW and EMF dependencies to create MD-SPLs and define a preliminary hierarchical folder structure to manage and centralize the core assets used to derive products. Then, architects can create and manage domain metamodels, feature models, and constraint models in a common repository, which captures and expresses the possible fine-grained variations affecting the product line. Product line architects also create transformation rules and decision models, which are transformed into (executable) model transformation workflows.

The automated production chain is implemented via model transformations and generated during domain engineering from the decision model. Its execution is realized during application engineering to derive a product. During application engineering, product designers use the variability identified and the core assets created during domain engineering, metamodels, feature models, models, and model transformation workflows to ensure the correct derivation of required products. Product designers create domain models and binding models, which must satisfy the constraint models previously created, to configure and derive products. Finally, designers execute the generated model transformation workflows using domain models and binding models as inputs, and transformation rules for processing the inputs.

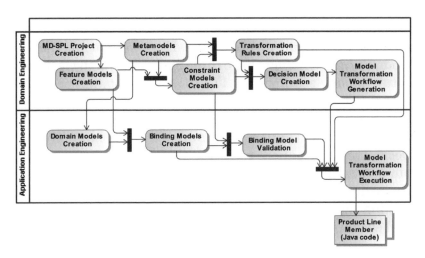

Figure 6.1. *Overview of our implementation strategy to create MD-SPLs*

6.3. The SPL of Smart-Home systems

The SPL we use through this chapter is the SPL of Smart-Home systems that was introduced in section 2.3.1. We present examples of diverse Smart-Home systems, which can be derived from the Small Building in Figure 6.2. To derive such Smart-Home systems, we re-use a common set of base and specific transformation rules that we developed as product line architects.

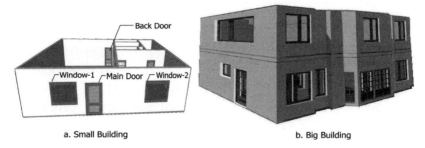

a. Small Building   b. Big Building

Figure 6.2. *Examples of buildings created by building architects*

Figure 6.3 presents the stages to configure and derive products. To configure diverse Smart-Home systems, on the one hand, *facilities designers* have three features from the facilities feature model (see Figure 4.11): Fingerprint, Keypad, and Automatic Windows. On the other hand, software architects have two features from the architecture feature model (see Figure 4.12): Periodic and Service. We have created specific transformation rules for deriving products, taking into account possible configurations the designers can create. For instance, we created one specific transformation rule for creating automatic windows. This transformation rule is re-used each time an automatic window is created.

In the second configuration stage (see Figure 6.3), facilities designers relate facilities to structural elements of buildings. For example, the Small Building can be configured to use Fingerprint in the Main Door as lock door control and Keypad in the Back Door. Similarly, each window can be individually configured as an Automatic or Manual Window. Table 6.1 presents the possible fine-grained configurations a facilities designer can create from the Small Building taking into account the variants Fingerprint, Keypad, and Automatic Windows. These are the 16 possible Smart-Home systems.

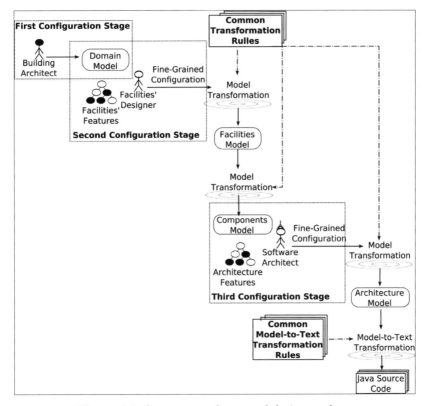

Figure 6.3. *Stages to configure and derive products*

Table 6.2 presents the possible configurations a designer can create taking into account only coarse-grained variations; for instance, the approaches in Chapter 4. In this case only four possible Smart-Home systems can be configured.

In the third configuration stage (see Figure 6.3), software architects relate software architecture variants to model elements representing software components. Table 6.3 presents the possible fine-grained configurations a software architect can create for the Smart-Home system from row one in Table 6.1 (SH-1), taking into account the variants Periodic and Service. There are four possible Smart-Home systems that can be configured. Thus, from the Small Building, taking into account the variants Fingerprint, Keypad, and Automatic Windows, and the variants Periodic and Service, product designers are able to configure 64 Smart-Home systems.

Smart-Home	Window-1	Window-2	Main Door	Back Door
SH-1	Automatic	Automatic	Keypad	Keypad
SH-2	Automatic	Automatic	Fingerprint	Fingerprint
SH-3	Automatic	Automatic	Keypad	Fingerprint
SH-4	Automatic	Automatic	Fingerprint	Keypad
SH-5	manual	manual	Keypad	Keypad
SH-6	manual	manual	Fingerprint	Fingerprint
SH-7	manual	manual	Keypad	Fingerprint
SH-8	manual	manual	Fingerprint	Keypad
SH-9	Automatic	manual	Keypad	Keypad
SH-10	Automatic	manual	Fingerprint	Fingerprint
SH-11	Automatic	manual	Keypad	Fingerprint
SH-12	Automatic	manual	Fingerprint	Keypad
SH-13	manual	Automatic	Keypad	Keypad
SH-14	manual	Automatic	Fingerprint	Fingerprint
SH-15	manual	Automatic	Keypad	Fingerprint
SH-16	manual	Automatic	Fingerprint	Keypad

Table 6.1. *Example of a fine-grained configuration for a Smart-Home system including Smart-Homes' facilities*

Table 6.4 presents the possible configurations a software architect can create for the Smart-Home system from row one in Table 6.1 (SH-1), taking into account the variants Periodic and Service, but considering only coarse-grained variations. In this case, product designers can only configure two different Smart-Home systems. Therefore, from the Small Building, taking into account the variants Fingerprint, Keypad, Automatic Windows, Periodic and Service, but considering only coarse-grained variations, product designers can configure only eight Smart-Home systems.

Smart-Home	Window-1	Window-2	Main Door	Back Door
SH-1	Automatic	Automatic	Keypad	Keypad
SH-2	Automatic	Automatic	Fingerprint	Fingerprint
SH-3	manual	manual	Keypad	Keypad
SH-4	manual	manual	Fingerprint	Fingerprint

Table 6.2. *Example of a coarse-grained configuration for a Smart-Home system including Smart-Homes' facilities*

Smart-Home	Window-1	Window-2	Main Door	Back Door	Windows Controller Component	Doors Lock Controller Component
SH-1.1	Automatic	Automatic	Keypad	Keypad	Periodic	Periodic
SH-1.2	Automatic	Automatic	Keypad	Keypad	Service	Service
SH-1.3	Automatic	Automatic	Keypad	Keypad	Periodic	Service
SH-1.4	Automatic	Automatic	Keypad	Keypad	Service	Periodic

Table 6.3. *Example of a fine-grained configuration for a Smart-Home system including software components' variants*

Smart-Home	Window-1	Window-2	Main Door	Back Door	Windows Controller Component	Doors Lock Controller Component
SH-1.1	Automatic	Automatic	Keypad	Keypad	Periodic	Periodic
SH-1.2	Automatic	Automatic	Keypad	Keypad	Service	Service

Table 6.4. *Example of a coarse-grained configuration for a Smart-Home system including software components' variants*

Using this small example, we showed how the concept of fine-grained configuration allows product designers to extend the scope of MD-SPLs. From eight Smart-Home systems that can be configured using coarse-grained configurations, we have shown how we can configure sixty four Smart-Home systems using the concept of fine-grained configuration. These fine-grained configurations satisfy the constraints defined in the constraint models of our application example, which capture the possible variability of the MD-SPL.

Regarding the derivation of the configured products, we created transformation rules that guarantee we can generate valid products from the fine-grained configurations. We define a valid product as an operable system that accomplishes the requirements that product designers specify by means of fine-feature configurations or binding models, which satisfy constraint models. However, considering the limitations presented in section 5.4, it was our responsibility as product line architects to create the transformation rules. Our approach does not yet provide mechanisms validating the transformation rules regarding the derivation of valid products from fine-grained configurations.

Figures 6.4 and 6.5 are examples of the GUI corresponding to one (fine-grained) configured Smart-Home System we derived. The Smart-Home system was configured to have one floor with two rooms, the Main Room and the Living Room. Figure 6.4 presents the Main Room, which has Air Conditioning as Environmental Control, and its door has Fingerprint as Door Lock Control. In this case, the product was configured to have the Air Conditioning Controller (software) component as a Service component. That is the reason why the air conditioning must be turned on/off manually.

Figure 6.5 presents the Living Room, which has Automatic Windows as Environmental Control, and its door has Keypad as Door Lock Control. The Living Room has three windows; two of them were (fine-grained) configured as Automatic Windows.

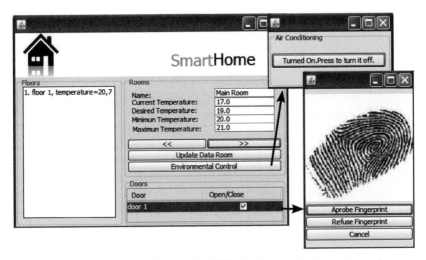

Figure 6.4. *Example 1 of the GUI of a fine-grained configured Smart-Home system*

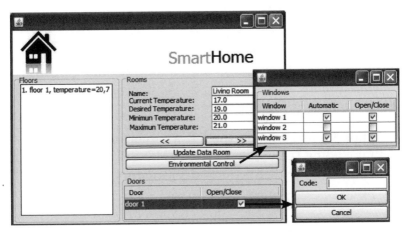

Figure 6.5. *Example 2 of the GUI of a fine-grained configured Smart-Home system*

Regarding the production cost, the highest cost to produce members of the Smart-Home MD-SPL is concentrated in the activities of core assets development (metamodels, feature models, transformation rules, and decision models), which are the responsibility of product line architects who must also be

MDE experts. However, we achieve a good return on investment since we obtain high quality in derived products and product designers invest little time in configuring products. Given that, the activities of product configuration are the responsibility of several (specialized) product designers, e.g. building architects, facilities designers, and software architects.

6.4. Variability expression and product configuration

This section presents the Eclipse plug-in tools devoted to the creation of a FieSta project and the various artifacts used to manage variability and to configure products.

6.4.1. *MD-SPL project creation*

We built an Eclipse plug-in that allows product line architects to create a particular type of Eclipse project. This type of project includes the required oAW and EMF dependencies to create MD-SPLs and define a hierarchical folder structure to manage and centralize the core assets associated to an MD-SPL project. We named this plug-in the *(MD-SPL) Project Creator*.

Figure 6.6 presents on the left a screenshot of the Eclipse menu including the option to create MD-SPL projects. On the right, Figure 6.6 presents the folder structure of an empty MD-SPL project.

6.4.2. *Metamodels and feature models creation*

In MDE, the metamodel creation is an important activity; this section describes the approach proposed by FieSta and also how to create specific feature models.

6.4.2.1. *Metamodels creation*

Once an MD-SPL project has been created, product line architects can create metamodels and feature models. Product line architects create metamodels by using MagicDraw [MAG 10], which is a UML 2 modeling tool that allows us to create UML Class Models and export them into UML 2 XMI files. Thus, from the UML 2 XMI files, product line architects generate Ecore models by using a component provided by oAW to transform UML 2 class models into Ecore models. Metamodels can also be created using Eclipse, EMF, or other UML editors that export to XMI files. The MD-SPL projects we create using our Project Creator plug-in include an oAW workflow file, which invokes the oAW component in charge of transforming UML 2 XMI files into Ecore models. To generate Ecore models, product line architects must meet the parameters for this oAW workflow file and then execute it to obtain the Ecore model. Therefore, we allow product line architects to create metamodels from a classic UML perspective, which facilitates the creation of domain metamodels.

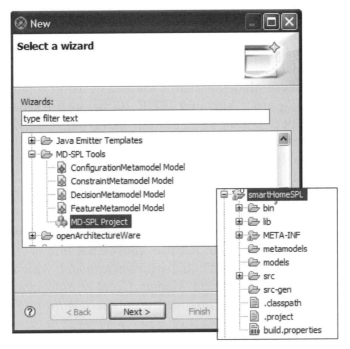

Figure 6.6. *Screenshot of the Project Creator plug-in*

Listing 6.1 presents an example of an oAW workflow file with parameters to generate Ecore models from UML 2 XMI files. In line 3, we define the location of the UML 2 model to be transformed. In line 4, we specify the target location of the resulting Ecore model. Line 5 to line 8 describes some additional properties required to perform the transformation.

```
1  <cartridge
2     file="org/openarchitectureware/util/uml2ecore/uml2ecoreWorkflow.oaw"
3     uml2ModelFile="..UML2Models∩domainMetamodel.uml2"
4        outputPath="..EcoreModels∩domainMetamodel.ecore"
5        nsUriPrefix="http://domainModel"
6        includedPackages="Data"
7        addNameAttribute="false"
8        resourcePerToplevelPackage="false"/>
```

Listing 6.1. *Example of an oAW workflow to generate metamodels from UML 2 XMI files*

6.4.2.2. *The feature models creator*

To create feature models, we provide the *Feature Models Creator*, which is an Eclipse plug-in. We decided to create our own Feature Models Creator instead of using commercial tools such as pure :: variants [PUR 10] or open source tools without support teams such as fmp [ANT 04]. Our Feature Models Creator includes a facility for preliminary validation of feature models. This plug-in validates that the lower bound of cardinality of features is minor or equal to the upper bound of cardinality of features, and solitary features have cardinality between zero and one; that is, the cardinality is *[0..1]* or *[1..1]*. To perform the validation of a feature model, we modified the Eclipse contextual menu that is related to files with extension *.featuremetamodel*, which is the extension that the Feature Models Creator associates with feature models. Thus, we provide the option to *Validate Feature Models Structure*, and we are able to present messages to inform the user if any inconsistency is found in a feature model.

6.4.2.3. *Metamodels and feature models for the SPL of Smart-Home systems*

In section [4.5] we introduced in detail the metamodels and feature models for our application example of the SPL of the Smart-Home systems (see from Figure 4.4 to Figure 4.12). Figure 6.7 presents the feature models created with the Feature Models Creator for this application example. The left side presents the facilities feature model and the right side describes the architecture feature model with classic tree views.

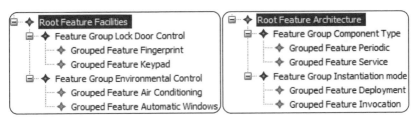

Figure 6.7. *Feature models for the SPL of Smart-Home systems*

6.4.3. *Constraint models creation*

This section presents the Constraint Model Creator and its use on the Smart-Home example.

6.4.3.1. *The constraint models creator*

We built an Eclipse plug-in to create constraint models, the *Constraint Models Creator*. Figure 6.8 presents the view associated with the Constraint Models Creator. The figure shows the creation of constraints between the domain metamodel and the facilities feature model from the SPL of our Smart-Home systems. Using our Constraint Models Creator, product line architects can load a metamodel and a feature model, create and delete constraints, clean up the workspace and then reload a new metamodel and a new feature model, and save a constraint model. The Constraint Models Creator allows for capturing the minimum and maximum cardinality that defines the constraint's cardinality property, and a description associated with the constraint.

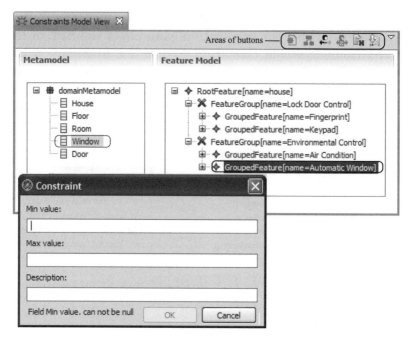

Figure 6.8. *Eclipse view of the constraint models creator*

When a product line architect chooses to save a constraint model, the plug-in performs two activities. First, it saves a file with extension *.constraint metamodel* containing the constraint model. Second, it saves a file with extension *.chk* that contains the Check expressions to validate binding models against the constraint model. Listing 6.2 presents an example of a Check expression generated by the Constraint Models Creator. The expression is generated from a constraint specifying that at least one Door element bound to the feature Lock Door Control has to exist in the binding model being validated.

Our current implementation of the Constraint Models Creator allows product line architects to create the *constraint properties* associated with constraints. This implementation does not allow, however, product line architects to create the *structural properties* associated with constraints. Therefore, the *structural properties* must be written directly on the Check files.

```
 1
 2  context  Binding ERROR loc ( )  +
 3     "There are less than 1 Door element bound "+
 4     "to the feature Lock Door Control" :
 5
 6     ( this . metaConcept  =  'Door '& &
 7     this . feature . parentFeature . name  =  'Lock Door Control '
 8     && (( Configuration ) this . eContainer ). binding ->
 9       select ( b | b . name=this . name  &&  this . metaConcept= 'Door '
10     && this . feature . parentFeature . name= 'Lock Door Control ').
11       size  >=  1);
```

Listing 6.2. *Example of a check file generated by the constraint models creator*

Listing 6.3 presents an example of a Check expression for a structural property. This is related to a constraint between the Component, metaconcept, and the feature Periodic. The structural property defines that only a Component element that is bound to the feature On Invocation can be bound to the feature Periodic. As part of our future work, we will allow product line architects to create the *structural properties* associated with constraints directly on the Constraint Models Creator.

```
 1
 2  context  Binding ERROR loc ( )  +
 3     "The Component "+ this . elementName +"must be "+
 4     "also bound to the  *On Invocation * feature ":
 5
 6     ( this . metaConcept  =  'Component ' &&
 7     this . feature . name  =  'Periodic '
 8     && (( Configuration ) this . eContainer ). binding ->
 9       select ( b | b . name=this . name  &&  this . feature . name=
10       'On Invocation '). size  =  1);
```

Listing 6.3. *Example of a check expression for a structural property*

In summary, our Constraint Models Creator allows product line architects to capture and express the variability described by possible fine-grained configurations, which we represent by using binding models, taking into account that fine-grained configurations have to be also restricted to represent valid products.

6.4.3.2. *Constraint models for the SPL of Smart-Home systems*

We create two constraint models for the SPL of our Smart-Home Systems. The first one is created between the domain metamodel and the facilities feature model. Table 6.5 presents these constraints that allow product line architects to capture and express the possible fine-grained variations between Smart-Home systems regarding domain and facilities concepts.

For example, product line architects can express that between one and two Doors can have Fingerprint as Lock Door Control in Smart-Home systems. As a result, product designers will be able to configure a Smart-Home system with one particular door having Fingerprint as Lock door control and another Smart-Home system with two selected doors having Fingerprint as Lock door control.

The second constraint model is created between the components metamodel and the architecture feature model. Table 6.6 presents these constraints, which allow product line architects to capture and express the possible fine-grained variations between Smart-Home systems regarding software components and software architecture concepts.

As a result, product line architects can express that in Smart-Home systems, for example, a component for managing Automatic Windows could be either a Service Component or a Periodic Component. Product designers will be able to configure a Smart-Home system with the component for managing Automatic Windows as a Periodic Component. This component will check the temperature of the room automatically where the automatic windows are used to open or close the windows. Another product designer will be able to configure a Smart-Home system with the component for managing Automatic Windows as a Service Component. In this case, the inhabitants must manually check the temperature of the room where the automatic windows are located. They must also manually activate the opening or closing of the windows.

Metaconcept	Feature	Cardinality	Description
Door	Lock Door Control	[0..1]	Doors can have either Fingerprint or Keypad or none of them as Lock Door Control
Door	Fingerprint	[1..2]	Between one and two Doors can have Fingerprint as Lock doorcontrol
Door	Keypad	[0..1]	Between zero and one Doors can have Keypad as Lock Door Control
Room	Environmental Control	[0..1]	Rooms can have either Automatic Windows or Air Conditioning or none of them as Environmental Control
Room	Automatic Windows	[1..1]	Only one Room can have Automatic Windows as Environmental Control
Room	Air Conditioning	[1..3]	Between one and three Rooms can have Air Conditioning as Environmental Control
Window	Automatic Windows	[0..4]	Between zero and four Windows can be Automatic Windows

Table 6.5. *Constraints between the domain metamodel and the facilities feature model*

Metaconcept	Feature	Cardinality	Description
Periodic	Component Type	[0..1]	Components classified as Periodic can be either Service or Periodic Components in the final software architecture
Component	Instantiation Mode	[1..2]	Components can be instantiated either On Deployment or On Invocation

Table 6.6. *(continued) Constraints between the components' metamodel and the architecture feature model*

6.4.4. *Domain models and binding models creation*

The fine-grained approach of FieSta requires the definition of several domain models and binding models to link the former with feature models describing variations. This section presents the process of creating domain and binding models and applies it to the Smart-Home case study.

6.4.4.1. *Domain models creation*

We built an Eclipse plug-in to create domain models using the facility provided by Eclipse to generate model editors from Ecore models. We named this plug-in the *Smart-Homes Domain Models Creator*. Product line architects have to create new domain metamodels and new domain model editors for producing new MD-SPLs.

Figure 6.9 presents a domain model created with our Smart-Homes Domain Models Creator. The model created by a *building architect* defines firstFloor and secondFloor. In the firstFloor there are two rooms, livingRoom, and kitchen. In the secondFloor, there is another room, mainRoom, which has two windows, mainRoomW1 and mainRoomW2. There are also two doors. The first door, livingRoomD1, is in the livingRoom. The second door, mainRoomD2, is in the mainRoom.

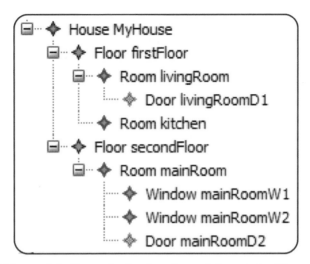

Figure 6.9. *Example of a domain model created with our Smart-Homes domain models creator*

6.4.4.2. *The binding models creator*

We developed an Eclipse plug-in named the *Binding Models Creator* to create binding models. Figure 6.10 presents the view associated with the Binding Models Creator. In this figure, we present the creation of bindings between the domain model and the facilities feature model from our Smart-Home systems SPL.

Using the Binding Models Creator, product designers can load a feature model, a domain model, and a constraint model, which will be used to validate the created binding model. Designers can create and delete bindings or select a feature. The facility to select features is useful when coarse-grained configurations are required. Therefore, we can select, for example, the automatic windows for all the windows in the house only by selecting the `Automatic Windows` feature.

When a product designer chooses to save a binding model, the plug-in performs two activities. First, it saves a file with extension *.configurationmetamodel* containing the binding model. Second, the binding model is validated against the constraint model loaded before. What really occurs is that the Check expressions generated from the constraint model are used to check the binding model to determine if it satisfies the constraints. After the validation, the product designer obtains messages informing him about the state of the validation.

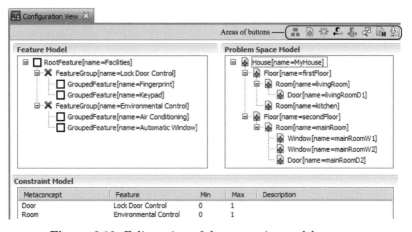

Figure 6.10. *Eclipse view of the constraint models creator*

In summary, our Binding Models Creator allows product designers to create fine-grained configurations by means of binding models. Our Binding Models Creator also allows product designers to validate the configurations against constraints expressing the valid fine-grained variations between products of the MD-SPL. This guarantees the configuration and subsequent derivation of valid products.

6.4.4.3. *Binding models for the SPL of Smart-Home systems*

Product designers can create several binding models, as well as domain models, to configure diverse Smart-Home systems of our MD-SPL. In the following section, we will present the process of configuring one particular Smart-Home system by creating the required binding models, which must satisfy the constraints presented before in Tables 6.5 and 6.6. The result will be a complete fine-grained configuration of a particular Smart-Home system of our MD-SPL.

Table 6.7 presents a set of bindings between the domain model from Figure 6.9 and our facilities feature model. These bindings are created by a *facilities designer*, and along with the domain model are part of the fine-grained configuration of the particular Smart-Home system we are configuring. They must satisfy the constraints presented in Table 6.6.

Element	Feature	Description
livingRoom	Air Conditioning	The livingRoom will manage Air Conditioning as Environmental Control
livingRoomD1	Fingerprint	The livingRoomD1 will manage Fingerprint as Lock Door Control System
mainRoomW1	Automatic Windows	The mainRoomW1 will be an Automatic Window
mainRoomD2	Keypad	The mainRoomD2 will manage Keypad as Lock Door Control system

Table 6.7. *Bindings between the domain model from Figure 6.9 and our facilities feature model*

According to this configuration, after the execution of the model transformation process, the product designer will obtain a particular Smart-Home system whose GUI is presented in Figures 6.11 and 6.12. Figure 6.11 shows the view associated with the mainRoom, which has one Automatic Windows, mainRoomW1, and its door, mainRoomD2, has Keypad as Lock Door Control mechanism.

Figure 6.12 presents the view associated with the livingRoom. In this case, the Air Conditioning is managed by a Periodic software component. That is the reason why the system automatically turns it on/off according to the desired temperature of the room. In this case the `Desired Temperature` of the `Living Room` is 19°C and the `Current Temperature` is 17°C, then the `Air Conditioning` is turned off. The door, `livingRoomD1`, has `Fingerprint` as `Lock Door Control` mechanism.

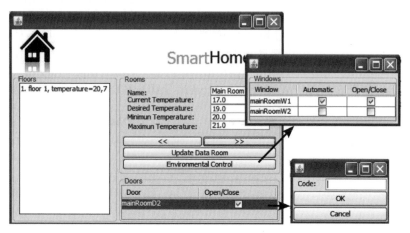

Figure 6.11. *View of the* `Main Room` *of the configured Smart-Home system*

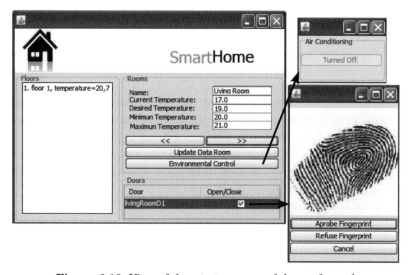

Figure 6.12. *View of the* `Living Room` *of the configured Smart-Home system*

Figure 6.13 presents the component's model derived from the domain model in Figure 6.9 given the bindings from Table 6.7. Product designers, who are software architects, have to create a binding model between this model of generated components and the architecture feature model. This binding model corresponds to the fine-grained configuration of the software components included in the Smart-Home system, and these bindings have to satisfy the constraints presented in Table 6.6.

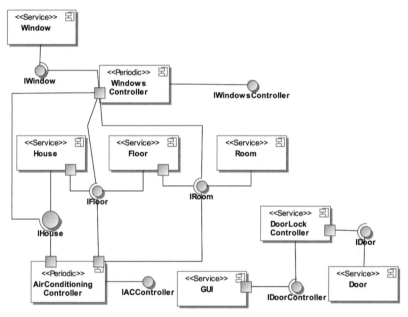

Figure 6.13. *Components' model derived from a domain model*

Table 6.8 presents a set of bindings between the components' model from Figure 6.13 and our architecture feature model. These bindings complete the required configuration to derive the Smart-Home system we are configuring. According to these bindings, the final architecture model for the Smart-Home system presented in Figures 6.11 and 6.12 will have only one `Periodic Component`, the `Air Conditioning Controller Component`. Furthermore, the `House` and

`Floor Components` will be instantiated on `Invocation`. The other components will be instantiated on `Deployment`.

Element	Feature	Description
Windows Controller	Service	The Windows Controller component will be a Service Component
Air Conditioning Controller	Periodic	The Air Conditioning Controller component will be a Periodic Component
House	Invocation	The House Component will be instantiated on Invocation
Floor	Invocation	The Floor Component will be instantiated on Invocation

Table 6.8. *Bindings between the components' model from Figure 6.13 and our architecture feature model*

6.5. Completing and running the product derivation

To automatically derive products with FieSta, we should create transformation rules and elaborate a decision model scheduling these rules according to the product configuration.

6.5.1. *Transformation rules creation*

In section 4.6, we introduced the several stages of model-to-model and model-to-text transformation rules for deriving configured Smart-Home systems.

Figure 6.14 presents a screenshot of the folder structure to maintain our model transformation rules. We use the Xpand and Xtend languages to create our transformation rules. These languages create files with extensions .xpt and .ext, respectively. We create two sets of transformation rules: the base and the specific ones. On the one hand, base transformation rules do not depend on any variant of the product line. Thus, they are always executed during the transformation process. On the other hand, we create specific transformation rules taking into account features that can affect the transformation process. Our transformation rules are organized in folders created for each transformation step.

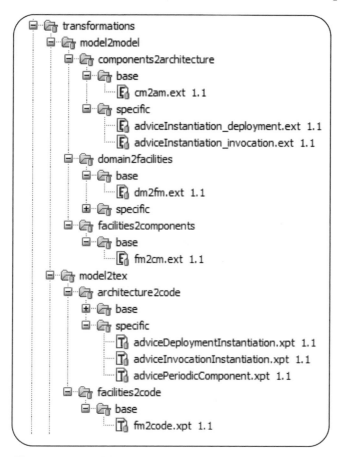

Figure 6.14. *Folder structure for transformation rules files*

Listing 6.4 presents a part of the model-to-text transformation rule to transform `Component` elements into Java source code. As was introduced in Chapter 5, we re-use pieces of code that have been previously tested to build complete OSGi implementations. The strategy is to use pre-built OSGi bundles and assemble them with the complete product line architecture. As a result, we guarantee the quality of derived Smart-Home systems. The source code in Listing 6.4 corresponds to the method we created to turn on the air conditioning located in a particular room.

```
1   "DEFINE_implementation_FOR_componentsMetamodel::Component_"
2   public void start(Integer floorId, Integer roomId)
3     throws Exception{
4
5     Room room = getRoom(floorId, roomId);
6     if(room != null && room.getEnvironmentalControl() ==
7       TypeEnvironmentalControl.AIRCONDITIONING){
8       room.setAirConditionStatus(true);
9     }
10  }
11  "ENDDEFINE"
```

Listing 6.4. *Model-to-text transformation rule to transform* Component *elements into Java source code*

6.5.2. *Decision models creation*

The decision is the main piece for running the production chain. This section explains how to create it and illustrates this with the Smart-Home example.

6.5.2.1. *The decision models editor*

We built an Eclipse plug-in to create decision models, the *Decision Models Editor*. This editor was developed using the Topcased facility to create model editors (see section 3.5) and is part of the contributions of the Master thesis of Andrés Romero [ROM 09].

Figure 6.15 presents the GUI of our Decision Models Editor. On the left, we present the palette of options to create Model-to-Model and Model-to-Text transformations, Base and Specific transformation rules, Aspects, Execution Conditions, CoarseConditions and FineConditions. Options also include the definition of the Source and Target models of the model transformations. On the right, we present part of the decision model created for our SPL of Smart-Home systems.

Our Decision Models Editor allows product line architects to maintain uncoupled i) the information of features, ii) the transformation rules, and iii) the possible execution conditions of transformation rules that particular feature configurations imply. Furthermore, our Decision Models Editor allows product line architects to capture, as independent Aspects, how transformation rules must be composed to derive configured products. This is a high-level mechanism, which is independent of the technology used to implement our approach. Finally, our plug-in can capture execution conditions of transformation rules to derive products based on binding models, which represent fine-grained configurations.

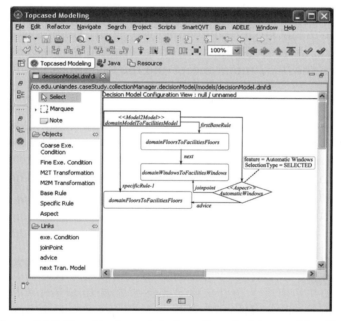

Figure 6.15. *Graphical user interface of our decision models editor*

6.5.2.2. *Decision models for the SPL of Smart-Home systems*

The decision models of our application example facilitate the derivation of any product that has been configured by creating i) a domain model, ii) a valid binding model between the facilities metamodel and the domain model, and iii) a valid binding model between the architecture metamodel and the component model derived from the domain model.

In section 4.6, we introduced part of the decision model we created for deriving configured Smart-Home systems. Similar to Figure 5.5, we defined an `Aspect` element related to each constraint in the two constraint models. As a result, we can guarantee that any binding satisfying a constraint will be taken into account during the derivation process. The model element involved in the binding will be transformed using a specific transformation rule in charge of transforming it according to the feature involved in the binding.

For instance, Figure 6.16 presents another part of the decision model for deriving configured Smart-Home systems. In this case, we present the `Aspect` we created for the constraint between the `Door` metaconcept and the `Fingerprint` feature. This `Aspect` specifies that any `Door` element in a binding model will be transformed using the specific transformation rule `doorToDoorWithFingerprint`. As a result, we can guarantee that any binding satisfying the constraint between the `Door` metaconcept and the `Fingerprint` feature will be taken into account to derive a Smart-Home system. The doors involved in the bindings will have fingerprint as lock door control mechanism.

6.5.3. *Generation and execution of model transformation workflows*

As we explained in Chapter 5, to execute our decision models, we need to transform them into executable oAW workflows by using a model-to-text transformation. This transformation is achieved using a model-to-text transformation, which is part of the Website [ARB]. As a result, we can execute the generated model transformation workflows on the model transformation engine of oAW. Thus, we derive any (fine-grained) configured product.

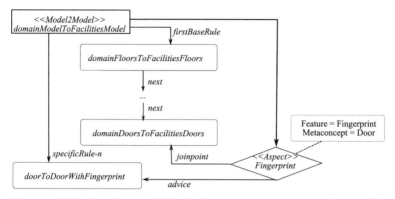

Figure 6.16. *Decision model including an aspect to derive doors with fingerprint as lock door control mechanism*

Figure 6.17 presents the final result of executing the sequence of model transformations we defined to generate a Smart-Home system of our product line. The files correspond to Java (OSGi) source code and XML descriptors, which have been generated departing from the domain model in Figure 6.9 and the binding models in Tables 6.7 and 6.8.

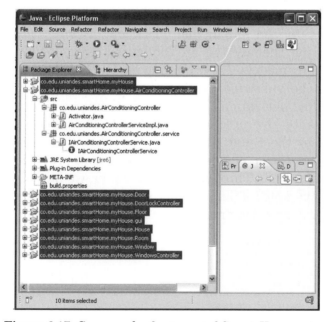

Figure 6.17. *Source code of a generated Smart-Home system*

We include on the Website [ARB], details about our entire tool support and the installation instructions. We also include all the core assets to create MD-SPLs of Smart-Home systems, such as the one we have used throughout this book to illustrate our approach. Additionally, we present another MD-SPL of stand-alone systems for managing collections, including all the required core assets to derive its product line members.

6.6. Summary

The FieSta toolkit is the set of tools we developed to support our MD-SPL engineering mechanisms to create SPLs. This chapter describes the Constraint Models Creator, the Feature Model Creator, the Binding Models Creator, and the Decision Models Editor. The FieSta process is represented as a UML activity diagram, which defines the various steps to create and to bind models during domain and application engineering. Once the MD-SPL is created, the user has to define metamodels, feature models, and constraint models at domain engineering. A subsequent step is to provide the transformation rules and the decision models that are required to generate the production workflow. During application engineering, the products are configured using domain models and binding models. These binding models link domain models and can be validated against the constraint models. Then, the product derivation can take place from the binding model and execute the production workflow. The entire chain is applied to the Smart-Home case study and illustrates the expressive power of fine-grained variations provided by the FieSta approach. Throughout this chapter, we have presented several examples of Smart-Home systems we derived using our MD-SPL engineering mechanisms and tool support.

Chapter 7

A Second Comprehensive Application Example

In this chapter, we present an application example that is related to stand-alone applications managing data collection. We call it a *collection manager system*, a product line member of this MD-SPL. For example, a collection manager system manages students from a school and their personal information: name, address, e-mail, etc. Another product manages discs in a music store and related information: name, artist, price, etc. This is a simpler example than the Smart Home, but its comprehensive presentation should help the reader to fully understand MD-SPL engineering.

7.1. Domain of the collection manager system

A collection manager is a kind of information system application devoted to the management (e.g. creation, storage, and query) of specific data from a business domain (e.g. school and university, employee management, music, or video store). Collection manager systems can be functionally represented and manipulated by data structures of type *Group*. A *Group* always has a main element that groups other elements. For example, in a music store application, it should be a *MusicStore Group* that assembles *Discs* and every *Disc* assembles *Songs*. Every element in the collection has a set of properties, and these properties are possibly related to other elements of the collection. Finally, each element is responsible for making its information persistent. Some of the functions that collection manager systems must provide include:

– *Create, Remove, Update, and Delete Elements*. These are generic facilities to manage elements in collections.

– *Organize, Filter, and Serialize Elements*. Elements in a collection must be organized according to several criteria to be presented to final users, for instance, alphabetical ordering of names, price ordering, etc. They can also be filtered for presentation to users or exported in several kinds of files.

– *Graphic Presentation of Elements*. Elements must be presented in different presentation views, such as tree, list, graph, or table.

These are only some sample functionalities considered in the second example. In this example, however, we could consider several other sources of variation, for example, performance issues of data management (memory and time consumption). Here, we simplify the problem and consider two dimensions: the kernel functionality, which allows us to vary the business domain (scholar, music store, or any kind of store, employees in a company, etc.) and the graphic presentation. Thus, we can deal with the usual range of classic variations we find in any kind of software applications managing data.

7.2. Requirements of the application example

For our particular application example, we characterize the product line of a collection manager system according to the following two sources of commonalities and two sources of variabilities associated with kernel functionality and user graphic presentation.

7.2.1. *Kernel commonalities*

The kernel manages data associated with instances of a business logic domain, such as *student* or *music store*. Thus, the business concept and its related characteristics can be represented using an aggregation structure. For example, a *student* assembles the set of characteristics: *code, name, address,* and *e-mail*. Any modeled business concept has a *name* characteristic and every product of the product line has functionality for adding data.

7.2.2. *GUI commonalities*

Graphical user interfaces use elements such as panels, lists, labels, and images, among others. All the GUI elements are grouped by different types of views. There are seven types of view that are mandatory for every product: (1) *main*, (2) *list*, (3) *information*, (4) *order*, (5) *filter*, (6) *exportation*, and (7) *creation* views; see Figure 7.1. The *main* view is in charge of communicating the kernel and the GUI by grouping all the other views. The *list* view displays data related to the *name* characteristic of created instances of the business logic concept. The *information* view is used to show the data related to all the characteristics of created instances of the business logic concept. The *order* view is used to select a characteristic that will be used as a reference for ordering the data displayed in the *information* and *list* views. The *filter* view is used to select a characteristic and a string of characters that will be used as the reference for filtering the data displayed in the *information* and *list* views. The *exportation* view is used to select the mechanism to export the data. The *creation* view is used to enter data for new instances of the business logic concept.

7.2.3. *Kernel and GUI variability*

– *Business Concept.* The most evident source of variation is the business concept and its characteristics. As we presented before, products can be created to manage data, such as *students, music stores,* or *address books.* Each concept may have several characteristics to describe it. Therefore, the configuration of the business concept and its characteristics must be performed by domain experts who are familiar with the data to be managed.

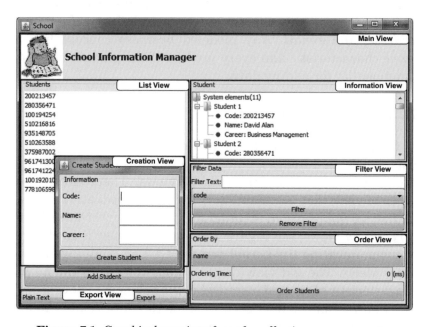

Figure 7.1. *Graphical user interface of a collection manager system*

– Ordering Data. We take into account the need to incorporate the facilities of a collection manager that are orthogonal to the selected business concept. The first one is the facility for ordering data in the collection. Elements in a collection must be organized according to several criteria to be presented to final users, for instance, alphabetical ordering of names or price ordering. A product may (or may not) provide functionality for ordering data. If it does, the data can be ordered using either the *bubble* or *insertion* algorithms. Thus, when products are configured, one ordering algorithm can be chosen to denote that every domain concept characteristic can be chosen for ordering data by using the selected algorithm,

which is a coarse-grained variation. For instance, if there exist two characteristics, *code* and *name*, and the *bubble* algorithm is selected, a product is generated where data can be ordered by *code* or *name* using the *bubble* algorithm. This characteristic can be also bound to optional domain concept characteristics that the designer has to select. For instance, a *name* characteristic can be bound to the *bubble* algorithm for ordering data or a *price* characteristic can be bound to the *insertion* algorithm. These are fine-grained variations between products.

– *Filtering Data.* Elements in a data collection can be filtered according to criteria based on domain concept characteristics to be presented to final users. Thus, data can be filtered, for instance, by *address* that matches some criteria. A product may (or may not) provide functionality for filtering data. If it does, data is filtered *removing* the elements that do not match the defined criteria. When products are configured, this facility can be chosen and bound to domain concept characteristics that the designer has to select. This allows a fine-grained variation between products. For instance, only the *Zip Code* characteristic can be used to be the base of a filter.

– *Managing Identifiers.* Domain concept characteristics can be selected to allow or disallow dealing with duplicate data. For instance, while managing a collection of songs, the *song duration* characteristic can be selected to allow duplicates; however, the *song name* characteristic can be selected to avoid duplicates. This allows you to have several songs with the same duration time but not with the same name. Thus, when products are configured, this facility can be chosen and bound to domain concept characteristics that the designer has to select, which allows fine-grained variations between products. For instance, as presented before, a *song name* characteristic can be selected to avoid duplicates.

– *Exporting Data.* Elements in a data collection can be exported in several formats. In our example, these formats are *plain* text, *Excel-type* files, or java *serialized* files. In the final product, the end-user has one format to export the data. Each product will be configured to allow the choice of the exporting format.

– *GUI Variability.* The product designer can select from several alternative views to present the data in the *information* view. The first one is a *simple* view with labels and text fields for each characteristic related to the domain concept managed by the product. Instances are displayed one-by-one. The second one uses a *grid* component. The grid component facilitates the display of many instances of the problem space concept at the same time. The third one uses a *tree* representation. Figure 7.1 presents the GUI of a collection manager system managing information of students and using a *tree* information view.

7.3. The overall process

According to our approach, we organize the lifecycle creation of MD-SPLs in a framework, FieSta, which incorporates the main principles of Model-Driven and SPL Engineering. There are two major processes on which our framework is focused: one is the process of capturing and expressing variability in MD-SPLs, which impacts consequently on the process of configuring product line members, and the other is the process of deriving products by re-using and composing model transformations based on product configurations. Figure 7.2 presents an activity diagram summarizing the processes involved in FieSta.

7.3.1. *Domain engineering*

During the domain engineering process, a product line architect creates metamodels, feature models, and constraint models to capture the variability and commonalities of MD-SPLs. As we have presented, constraint models make it possible for product line architects to capture and express the valid fine-grained variations between product line members by using the concepts of *constraint, cardinality property,* and *structural dependency property*. During the domain engineering process, product line architects create model transformations that implement algorithms to transform application domain models into refined models or source code. Product line architects also create decision models. Decision models capture the execution ordering of transformation rules to be performed by the model transformation engine to derive configured products.

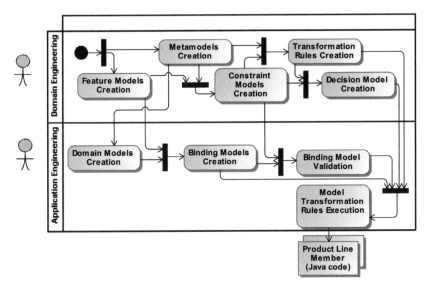

Figure 7.2. *General process*

7.3.2. *Application engineering*

To configure a product during the application engineering process, product designers create Models, which conform to metamodels created at domain engineering, and binding models, which denote fine-grained variations. After a binding model is created, we validate this against a set of OCL sentences derived from its respective constraint model. To derive a complete product according to a binding model, we dynamically adapt the parameters of model transformation executions. We achieve it using model transformation rules, which are selected from the binding model and the pre-created decision models.

7.4. Variability expression and product configuration

As presented previously, playing the role of product line architects, we use metamodels and feature models as our base core assets to capture and express variability; playing the role of product designers, we configure products by creating models that conform to metamodels and binding models.

7.4.1. Metamodels

In FieSta, we use a multi-staged approach for configuration and derivation of products. To create the product line of collection manager systems, we create metamodels playing the role of product line architects. The first metamodel we built as product line architects is the *problem space metamodel*, which serves to define the domain concept we want to manage and its characteristics. *Problem Space* models, which are created by product designers, do not include GUI concepts or details of functionality. Other metamodels contain GUI and functionality concepts, which are orthogonal to the domain concept chosen to be managed. Every metamodel plays a different role during the product line development lifecycle. The first metamodel is used by designers during the configuration process to create domain models, which are the starting point to derive collection manager systems. The other two metamodels capture the sources of variability that characterize our product line:

– *Problem Space Metamodel.* This metamodel includes concepts regarding the domain concept to be managed and its characteristics.

– *Kernel Metamodel.* Every system has functionalities according to product user choices; the kernel metamodel allows us to model variable products from the end-user functionality point of view.

– GUI Metamodel. This metamodel includes only concepts concerning the user interface. This metamodel represents the domain concept and its characteristics in terms of graphical elements.

In the same way as the Smart-Home example, it is also possible to create other metamodels to represent other viewpoints involved in the development of product line members. In this case study, however, we limit the viewpoint division to the metamodels we described before in order to have a comprehensive example.

Figure 7.3 presents the transformation steps processed on a model conforming to the problem space metamodel from its creation until the production of the source code application. The model transformation rules are used in three stages, each one with a dedicated set of rules. The first set of rules is defined from the problem space metamodel to the `Kernel` metamodel. The second set is defined from the problem space metamodel to the `GUI` metamodel. Finally, the third set of transformation rules includes model-to-text transformations, which produce the source code of product line members. We create model-to-text transformation rules from the `Kernel` and the `GUI` metamodels to Java source code. The following sections present details about the model transformations, and the possible variations these model transformations can have according to the SPL variability.

Problem Space Metamodel. The first metamodel is the `Problem Space` metamodel, which includes the domain concept and their characteristics. Figure 7.4 presents this metamodel (left) and an example of a domain model (right). The model defines a `student` element, which conforms to `Concept`. Every `student` is characterized by their characteristics: `code`, `name`, `address` and `e-mail`, which conforms to `Characteristic` .

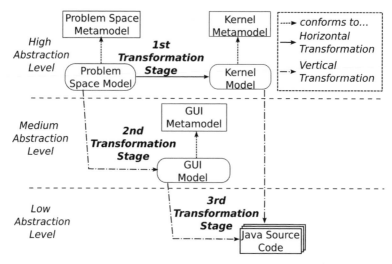

Figure 7.3. *Staged-transformations to derive collection manager systems*

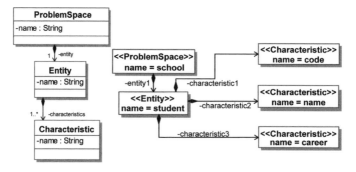

Figure 7.4. *Problem space metamodel and a model example*

Kernel Metamodel. This metamodel is at the same level of abstraction as the Problem Space metamodel. Similar to the Problem Space metamodel, the Kernel metamodel includes the domain concept to be modeled and its characteristics. In addition, it includes concepts to represent the possible variations regarding filters to be applied on data (Filter), sorting algorithms to present data (Sort, and

`AlgorithmSort`), and the characteristic of every attribute that indicates if data can be duplicated (`isIdentifier`). Figure 7.5 presents the `Kernel` metamodel. Models that conform to this metamodel are generated from `Problem Space` models in our defined staged-transformation chain. Product designers do not take place in the manual creation of `Kernel` models. Designers configure resulting kernel models by selecting features from the feature model we present in Figure 7.7.

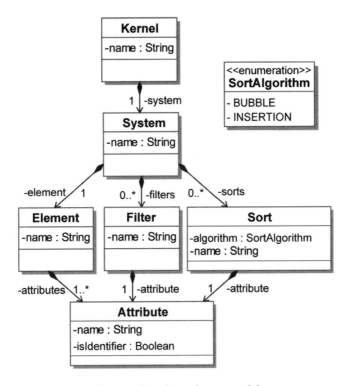

Figure 7.5. *Kernel metamodel*

GUI Metamodel. The `GUI` metamodel represents the graphical user interface viewpoint. This metamodel is at a lower abstraction level than the `Problem Space` and `Kernel` metamodels. Every concept in the metamodel represents a type of `View`, all of them grouped by the `MainView`. The `InfoView` is specialized by the `InfoSingleView`, `InfoGridView` and

InfoTreeView. This allows us to create GUI models where the information view varies. Figure 7.6 presents the GUI metamodel. Models that conform to this metamodel are generated from Problem Space models. Similarly, as in the Kernel model, product designers do not take part in the manual creation of this model. Designers configure resulting GUI models by selecting features from the feature model we present in Figure 7.7.

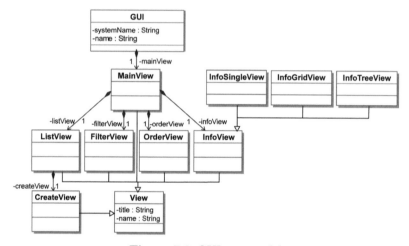

Figure 7.6. *GUI metamodel*

7.4.2. *The feature model*

In FieSta, we allow product designers to configure a product by giving a starting model, a Problem Space model in this example, and creating a binding model that satisfies a constraint model. To create binding models and constraint models, we have to first define a feature model. For this example, playing the role of product line architects, we create only one feature model that represents the variants of collection manager applications that are not represented in the Problem Space metamodel.

As was introduced in section 7.2.3, we take into account the need for incorporating facilities to the collection manager

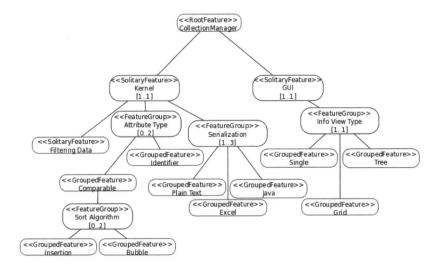

Figure 7.7. *Collection manager feature model*

applications that are orthogonal to the domain concept and its characteristics. Figure 7.7 presents our feature model. The `Kernel` feature, which is a solitary one, has two group features, `AttributeType` and `Serialization`. `AttributeType` groups the three variations that can be applied to characteristics, `FilteringData`, `Identifier`, and `Comparable`. These variations are used to create constraint models to express that, for instance, one or several characteristics can be selected as the base the for `FilteringData`; one or several characteristics can be used to define the uniqueness of one record over the complete data by means of an `Identifier`, which is also a fine-grained variation; one or several `Comparable` characteristics can be used to sort the data by using one of the available algorithms, `Bubble` or `Insertion`. Features grouped by the `Attribute Type` feature are able to define fine-grained variations between products; that is, features grouped by the `Attribute Type` feature can be bound to particular characteristics one-by-one.

Serialization groups the three variations for exporting data, PlainText, Excel, and standard Java serialization. These variants represent a coarse-grained variation, which means that only by selecting one of the features in a configuration, the generation of a product follows a general pattern. In this case, for instance, if a product designer selects the feature PlainText, a product exporting data to plain text will be created.

The GUI feature, which is a group, groups the three variations for creating the information view, Grid, Single, and Tree. This is also a coarse-grained variation. For instance, if a product designer selects the feature Grid, a product with a grid as information view will be created.

7.4.3. *The constraint model*

Playing the role of product line architects, we create constraint models to restrict the bindings among model elements and features; for example, to express that only problem space models can be bound to our feature model, or that maximum two Characteristic elements can be bound to the feature FilteringData. We can also say that constraint models restrict the fine-grained variations allowed between product line members. Our constraints serve to avoid inconsistencies during the configuration and derivation processes.

Figure 7.8 presents our constraint model for this example. We define a constraint between the Characteristic metaconcept and the FilteringData feature, constraint1= [Characteristic , FilteringData , [0..*], true]. The constraint describes that during the configuration of a product, product designers can bind undetermined Characteristic elements; for example, the code, with the feature FilteringData (see Figure 7.9). Then, each bound element could be used as a filter in the final product.

The constraint between the `Characteristic` metaconcept and the `Attribute Type` feature, `constraint2=` [`Characteristic`, `Attribute Type`,[0..2], *true*], describes that product designers can bind `Characteristic` elements with the `Identifier` feature, the `Comparable` feature, or both of them. Then on the one hand, elements in the collection could be unique in terms of one characteristic; for instance, if a `code` characteristic is an `identifier`, then it is not possible to have two elements in the collection with the same code. On the other hand, elements in the collection could be ordered using one sort algorithm as described by the `constraint3`.

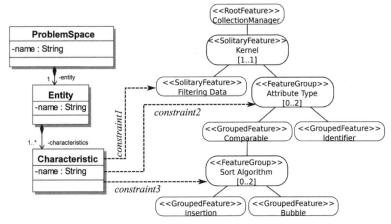

Figure 7.8. *Collection manager constraint model*

The `constraint3` = [`Characteristic`, `Sort Algorithm`, [0..2], *true*], describes that product designers can bind `Characteristic` elements with the `Insertion` feature, the `Bubble` feature, or both of them. Then, elements in the collection could be ordered using the characteristic and any of the available sort algorithms.

7.4.4. *Binding models*

Product designers create binding models to configure products. That is, binding models capture fine-grained variations between products. A binding is a relationship between a model element and a feature. For example, to express that the code is used for FilteringData, $B = [\text{code},$ FilteringData$]$.

Figure 7.9 presents our binding model for this example. This binding model is created between the problem space model from Figure 7.4 and the feature model from Figure 7.7. binding1 configures the code characteristic for filtering data. binding2 denotes the code characteristic as an Identifier, which means that two records with the same code cannot exist in the collection manager. binding3 and binding4 configure the name characteristic as a base for ordering data by using the Insertion algorithm. binding5 and binding6 configure the career characteristic as a base for ordering data by using the Bubble algorithm.

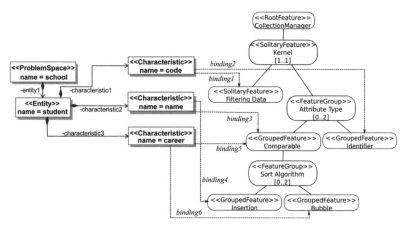

Figure 7.9. *Collection manager binding model*

Figure 7.10 summarizes the processes of (1) expressing the variability in our application example SPL and (2) configuring a collection manager system. First, a product designer creates a Problem Space Model based on the Problem Space metamodel. Then, the designer creates a binding model based on the feature model and the problem space model. The binding model affects the transformation of the `Problem Space Model` into the `Kernel Model`. According to created bindings in the case of fine-grained variations and selected features in the case of coarse-grained variations, particular transformation rules must be executed to create kernel models.

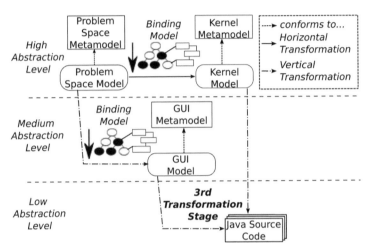

Figure 7.10. *Summary of the configuration process of the collection manager systems*

7.5. Core assets development and product derivation

We introduced metamodels, feature models, and constraint models as the core assets we use to express variability. In FieSta, we use model transformation rules as the main core assets to derive product line members. In the next subsections we present: the transformation rules and software artifacts we created for our second application example and the decision model we built to derive products.

7.5.1. *Rule transformations in the SPL of the collection manager systems*

As we introduced before (see Figure 7.3), the transformation rules we created for our application example are used in three stages. The first set of rules is defined from the problem space metamodel to the `Kernel` metamodel. The second set is defined from the problem space metamodel to the `GUI` metamodel. These are created taking into account our constraint model. The third set of transformation rules includes model-to-text transformations, which produce the source code of product line members.

First Stage: Problem space-to-kernel transformation rules. The purpose of these transformation rules is adding information about collection manager facilities to problem space models. These are horizontal model-to-model transformations. It means they transform models inside the same abstraction level, the application domain abstraction level, but add concerns related to collection manager facilities.

We created two sets of transformation rules: the *base* and the *specific* ones. For instance, we create a base transformation rule to transform `ProblemSpace::Entity` elements into `Kernel::Element` elements. Similarly, we created a base transformation rule to transform `ProblemSpace::Characteristic` elements into `Kernel::Attribute` elements. We created specific transformation rules taking into account the possible bindings that can affect the transformation process. For instance, we created two specific transformation rules to transform `ProblemSpace::Characteristic` elements; the first one, taking into account the `constraint1` (see Figure 7.8), creates `Kernel::Filter` elements for each `Characteristic` bound to the `FilteringData` feature in the binding model; the second one, taking into account the `constraint3`, creates `Kernel::Sort` elements for each `Characteristic` bound to one of the `Sort Algorithm` (grouped) features in the binding model.

Second Stage: Problem space-to-GUI transformation rules. The second set of transformation rules is defined from the problem space metamodel to the `GUI` metamodel. These are vertical model-to-model transformations since they transform models between different abstraction levels. The source abstraction level is the application domain abstraction level, whereas the target level is the abstraction level including concerns related to GUI components.

We created base transformation rules to create the common views in the GUI of a collection manager system. We created three specific transformation rules to create GUI:InfoSingleView, GUI:InfoGridView, and GUI:InfoTreeView. In this case, since these are coarse-grained variants, which means that the selection of a feature guides the derivation process without taking into account model elements, these three transformation rules are created based only on the feature model without taking into account either the constraint or the binding models. Thus, for instance, if the Single feature is selected, one GUI:InfoSingleView element is created.

Third Stage: Model-to-text transformation rules. The model-to-text transformation rules produce the source code of product line members. These transformation rules have as input a kernel model and a GUI model. The transformation rules are in charge of creating Java classes at the kernel and GUI layers to connect them.

7.5.2. *Decision models*

We explained that we create specific transformation rules taking into account the possible bindings in binding models, which satisfy constraints in constraint models. That is, taking into account fine-grained variations. We need a mechanism for selecting and executing automatically the base transformation rules and only some specific transformation rules associated to fine-grained variations. We proposed the use of explicit *decision models* for composition of transformation rules based on binding models, which implies the modification of a baseline scheduling taking into account not only features from feature configurations, but also bindings from binding models.

Thus, for instance, if any `Characteristic` element is bound to the feature `FilteringData` in a binding model, the base sequence to transform problem space models into kernel models must be modified. This modification implies the replacement of the rule `characteristicToAttribute` by the rule `charactericteToFilterAttribute`. This rule must transform only the `ProblemSpace::Characteristic` elements that are bound to the `FilteringData` feature, into `Kernel:Filter` elements. For instance, from the binding model presented in Figure 7.8, given that the `code` element in the problem space model is the only characteristic bound to the `FilteringData` feature, this is the only characteristic that must be transformed into a `Filter` element in the kernel model.

Figure 7.11 presents a small part of our decision model to transform problem space models into kernel models taking into account binding models. We can see in the figure that we first define a baseline scheduling, which includes the execution of the transformation rules `problemSpaceToSystem`, `entityToElement`, and `characteristicToAttribute`. Then, we create an aspect indicating that if some bindings satisfy `constraint1` (which describes that product designers can bind `Characteristic` elements with the feature `FilteringData`) the execution of the base transformation rule `characteristicToEntity` must be intercepted. After the interception is done, the specific transformation rule `charactericteToFilterAttribute` must be then executed. This rule queries the binding model used to configure the product, which is derived, and transforms only the `Characteristic` elements bound to the `FilteringData` feature.

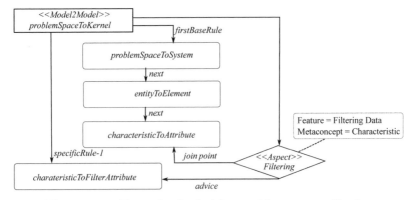

Figure 7.11. *Example of a decision model to create collection manager systems with binding models*

7.6. Summary

In this chapter, we presented a second application example related to stand-alone applications managing data collections. We call this a *collection manager system*, a product line member of this MD-SPL. A collection manager is devoted to the management of specific data from a business domain. We presented the commonalities and variability involved in the product line along with the metamodels, the feature model, and the constraint model we created to capture such commonality and variability. We presented as an example some parts of a binding model we created as a means to configure a product line member, and we presented also parts of the decision model we used to generate operable systems. We explained the staged process to generate a collection manager system, from the creation of a problem space model, through the configuration of the variations chosen for product designers, until the final generation of a product.

Chapter 8

Further Reading

This chapter is devoted to additional references and discussions. It first introduces some of the main books related to the topics of product lines and model engineering. We discuss more precisely feature modeling, decision modeling, MD-SPL approaches, dynamic variability, and domain- specific modeling. Some complementary topics and references are presented to advise the reader about future trends close to MD-SPL engineering.

8.1. Northop and Clements' book

Northop and Clements' book is a summary of the fundamentals on software product lines that presents explanations of the fundamental concepts and describes three case studies. The authors define and explore the core activities for development of software product lines and discuss specific practice areas in engineering, technical management, and organizational management. For example, defining the architecture is a software engineering practice area; configuration control is a technical management practice area; and training is an organizational management practice area. Methods to develop a re-usable base of core assets and to develop products that use those core assets are also discussed. To help organizations to develop SPLs, the book describes 29 practice areas that must be mastered. This book, however, presents an academic point of view; it lacks real industry problems. The authors succeed in presenting a pattern catalog for SPLE. The catalog includes, for instance, each asset pattern, build pattern, product parts pattern, assembly line pattern, product builder pattern, cold start pattern, process pattern, and factory pattern.

8.2. Pohl, Böckle and Van der Linden's book

The book from Pohl *et al.* [POH 05b] gives a general view and the foundations of SPLE, but it does not address MDE techniques. It is an important work as it clearly defines the concepts and the processes involved in product line engineering. It covers most of the questions raised by this engineering: variability modeling, documentation, testing, requirements engineering, and traceability. Each process, domain and application engineering, are split into four stages: requirements, design, realization, and testing, which gives a strong consistency to the approach. One chapter is dedicated to variability management. The book argues for an orthogonal variability model and explains how to document variability in artifacts. It also presents two key organizational aspects not covered at all in our book. Traceability is mentioned as an important aspect in SPLE, but there is no part summarizing a precise methodology to follow.

8.3. Gomaa's book

The *Designing Software Product Lines with UML* [GOM 04] proposes an extension of UML 2.0 to cope with software families. It presents a UML-based analysis and design method and uses the model-driven architecture concepts to develop component-based software for product lines. As such, this is a practical and seamless approach to switch to SPLE. The method PLUS described in the book proposes a set of concepts to extend UML notations with variability. The extended diagrams are use cases, static, state machines, and interaction diagrams. These classic UML diagrams are enriched to address commonalities and variabilities. A feature modeling view, based on a static class diagram, is proposed to capture commonalities and variabilities at the requirements level. An additional view is devoted to the implementation dependencies between the feature diagram and the static diagram. The book also introduces architectural patterns to develop re-usable component architectures. The scope of the book is restricted to traditional software development with UML and explores the adaptation of the Unified Development Software Process to address software product lines. One of the most original parts of the book is the extension of state charts leading to dynamic variability. One chapter is dedicated to the comprehensive description of three case studies.

8.4. Van der Linden, Schmid, and Rommes' book

The book [LIN 07] addresses a survey of product line practices and is a valuable reference for practitioners who want to launch a product line. The book first introduces general concepts about SPLE and the main processes. One important point is that it covers business and organizational concerns and shows that they are important for the success of any SPL project. It thoroughly reviews the most important points and argues that the model's business, architecture, process, and organization are suitable to manage product line engineering. It also provides a framework to evaluate an SPL organization based on the CMMI model. Part 2 of the book summarizes ten different examples of SPL realizations, covering various domains and different companies and business organizations. Thus, the book exposes some guidelines to having a successful SPLE but also some problems and examples of real benefits of using SPLE. The last part is devoted to a summary and analysis of the results gained from the SPL examples. One chapter focuses precisely on the question of introducing SPLE and proposes a ten-step approach.

8.5. Stahl, Voelter, and Czarnecki book

Model-Driven Software Development: Technology, Engineering, Management [SVC 06a] is a complete guide for MDE practitioners. Part 1 of the book presents an overview of the approach: terminology, history, and classification in the generative development field, and at the time of its creation (2006), the status of the MDE practice. The authors also present in detail the case study of a typical Web application with all the challenges it overcomes, which helps the reader understand the real context of software development. The second part of the book introduces concepts regarding domain-specific modeling by means of metamodels and UML-based techniques. Software architectures are specially treated in this part in order to illustrate the applicability of MDE. A deep discussion of MDE in the context of code generation techniques is presented along with a broad classification of such techniques. The third part of the book centers on the processes involved in MDE projects and presents two new case studies to illustrate a full MDE process chain. The fourth section covers economic and organizational topics. The return of investment on MDE is evaluated, roles and skills are defined for practitioners, and strategies for MDE adoption are discussed.

8.6. AMPLE book

The results of the AMPLE project[1] were published in a book [RAS 11]. This European project aimed at combining state-of-the-art in aspect-oriented software development and

---

1 http://www.ample-project.net/.

MDE to advance software product line engineering. Currently, there is a big gap between research in requirements analysis, architectural modeling, implementation technology, and the industrial practice in SPL engineering. The focus of current approaches is mainly on the design and code level while the variations still need to be identified, managed, and analyzed from the very early stage of requirements engineering. Architecture models are linked to requirements in an *ad-hoc* fashion and implementations are pre-processed, which are inadequate substitutes for proper programming language support for variability. There is no systematic traceability framework for relating variations across an SPL engineering lifecycle.

The AMPLE book provides a holistic view of SPLE and proposes several advances in this domain. The first one is about the analysis of requirements to produce a feature model in an assisted way. The partners of the project have also elaborated a general language for variability modeling and one Java extension enabling feature-oriented programming. One specific effort has been made on traceability, which is cutting across all the SPL activities. In a complex software process such as SPLE, it could be beneficial to have techniques and tools to analyze design rationale and to support non-functional requirements.

The book provides several chapters dedicated to SPLE and MDE with concrete examples. Most of these researches were implemented in tools and experimented with on case studies. A general tool chain was designed covering both solution and product-oriented product lines. This general approach uses model-driven engineeringand aspect-oriented programming, but can be "forked" in two different MD-SPL chains, namely TENTE and MAPLE. TENTE proposes a way where automatic derivation from the feature model is increased, but it required the use of an advanced programming language incorporating facility for feature-oriented programming. Thus, more variability could be left open until source code compilation or runtime execution. MAPLE does not require such an advanced programming language and relies only on traditional programming language. Variability is often managed by successive model transformations before source code generation. We have to mention that the approach we present in this book was developed also in the context of the AMPLE project.

8.7. Feature modeling notations

Feature modeling is a method and notation for capturing commonalities and variabilities in product lines [KAN 90, KAN 98, RIE 02, CZA 05, VÖL 07b]. Features describe the common and variable functionality of a system under development. Feature modeling was first introduced by Kang *et al.* as FODA [KAN 90]. FODA is described as a domain analysis method for identifying prominent and distinctive features of a set of systems in a specific domain. In FODA, the features are used to define a specific domain in terms of its *mandatory, optional,* or *alternative* characteristics. After Kang *et al.*, other authors extended the concepts regarding feature modeling. Among these extensions are the concepts of feature cardinality [CZA 00], groups and group cardinality [RIE 02], and attributes for features [CZA 02] among others. The purpose of these extensions is to restrict the set of variants that can be selected from feature models to create particular configurations. One of the most cited works on feature modeling is presented by Czarnecki *et al.* [CZA 04], where the authors propose a *cardinality-based* notation for feature modeling including *solitary, group,* and *grouped* features. This approach integrates a number of existing extensions; thus we suggest the use of this notation.

8.8. Decision models

Decision models were introduced to capture variability and to help in deriving products [ATK 00, BAY 00]. Product line architects create decision models during domain engineering. Decision models are used during application engineering as the main artifacts to assist in the product derivation. Decision models, as used in [ATK 00, BAY 00, FOR 08, DHU 08], are intended to close the gap between variability at a conceptual level (variation points and variants) and variability at the implementation level (concrete core assets). Bayer *et al.* [BAY 00], in the PuLSE approach, use decision models as a means to realize domain and architecture decision. Many authors have been now exploiting this notion, such as [ZIA 06] who designed it with the abstract factory pattern. [FOR 08] present decision models as a means for dealing with software variability and views on decision models that are supposed to help in variability management. Some mechanisms for supporting the process of decision modeling and resolving decision models have been introduced. In general terms, every SPL approach based on MDE introduces a form of decision model or similar artifacts in order to assist the derivation process (see Chapter 4). For instance, Wagelaar's approach [WAG 05, WAG 08a, WAG 08b] uses *platform dependency constraints* and superimposition variants, an ATL facility, in order to assist the derivation process; Loughran *et al.*'s approach [LOU 08, SAN 08], defines a language to capture variability and decision models.

MDE and AOP provide good opportunities to automate the product derivation, thus improving greatly the production chain. We propose the use of explicit decision models in the context of MDE as a mechanism for composition of transformation rules based on feature configurations [ARB 09]. This mechanism can be used in conjunction with transformation languages, which provide facilities to compose transformation rules. One of the strengths of our approach is that it provides a model-based strategy for defining decision models. It can be, thus, the base of a platform independent strategy. In particular, we used the oAW modeling framework and the Xtend and Xpand model transformation languages, which provide a mechanism based on AOP for the composition of transformation rules (see section 3.6.4). Decision models are the base of our mechanism to derive products including variability. They capture the execution ordering of transformation rules to be performed by the model transformation engine to derive configured products. We use aspect-oriented programming, provided by oAW, to build the scheduling of the transformation rules, i.e. the ordering in which transformation rules are going to process model elements to accomplish the desired derivation.

8.9. Model-driven software product lines

MD-SPL are product lines created based on MDE principles (see Chapter 4). A product line member of an MD-SPL is created from an application domain model that (1) conforms to an application domain metamodel and (2) is transformed until obtaining the application by using model-to-model and model-to-text transformations. There is no reference framework for creating MD-SPLs. For many in this domain (e.g. [VÖL 07b]), including us [ARB 09a, ARB 09b], these model transformations may require several stages and may include horizontal and vertical transformations. At each transformation stage, application domain models are automatically transformed to include new concerns from a particular abstraction level or more implementation details from lower abstraction levels.

Several approaches to create SPLs have emerged that are based on MDE. In this section, we discuss four of the most *representative* works presented in the area. These approaches are Czarnecki and Antkiewicz's approach [CZA 05], Wagelaar's approach [WAG 05, WAG 08a, WAG 08b], Loughran *et al.*'s approach [LOU 08, SAN 08], and Voelter and Groher's approach [VÖL 07b]. We have chosen to present each work following two aspects, see Figure 8.1. The first one, located in the *problem space* [CZA 00], is related to the mechanisms the approaches use for expressing variability and configuring products. The second one, located in the *solution space* [CZA 00], is related to the core assets development and the mechanisms for deriving products. These two aspects deserve our attention since they are at the core of the research problems exposed in this book, which we aim to resolve with our proposal (Chapter 5).

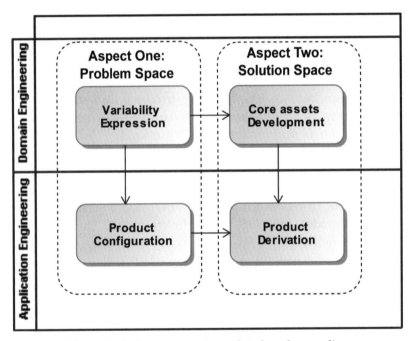

Figure 8.1. *Aspects to review related work regarding model-driven software product lines*

At the end of this section, we present a discussion emphasizing the advantages and drawbacks of the different mechanisms used by the presented approaches. We did not list other valuable references like [ZIA 06, ATK 00, BAY 99, PUR 10] since they are subsumed by the four presented here, or are discussed in other parts of this book, or are commercial approaches without available full documentation.

8.9.1. *The Czarnecki and Antkiewicz's approach*

8.9.1.1. *Problem space: expressing variability and configuring products*

To express variability, Czarnecki and Antkiewicz [CZA 05] propose an approach where variation points and variants are captured by means of feature models. They extend the FODA approach by adding cardinality and attributes for features. Products are configured by creating feature configurations.

8.9.1.2. *Solution space: core assets development and products derivation*

The main core assets built by product line architects to derive products in Czarnecki and Antkiewicz's approach are *template models* and model transformations.

Template models are expressed using UML and represent all the possible elements required to create product line members. For example, to represent a family of UML 2.0 activity models, both the model template and the template instances are expressed using the UML 2.0 activity modeling notation. A template model is a superimposition of all the possible model elements required to derive diverse products according to feature configurations.

Template models are annotated by product line architects using *presence conditions* and *meta-expressions*. The annotations are defined in terms of features from a feature model, which capture the variability of the product line under development. Presence conditions indicate whether an element should remain in or be removed from a template instance because of the presence of a particular feature in feature configurations. Meta-expressions indicate how to compute attributes of model elements, such as the name of an element or the return type of an operation, based on values assigned to feature attributes in feature configurations.

Product line architects also create model-to-model transformations to instantiate the template models automatically and thus to derive configured product line members. In these model-to-model transformations, both the input and output models conform to the UML 2.0 metamodel. Several model transformations are created; each one is in charge of removing elements from the template model and/or computing attributes of model elements according to the annotations in the template model. Thus, based on a feature configuration, a template model can be instantiated automatically by using model transformations.

Decision models are not explicitly created to support the product derivation process. The resolution of variability is performed by product designers creating feature configurations. However, the *effects* on UML models are specified in the model annotations. This produces high coupling between the core assets and the required *effects* to create products.

Thus, products are derived from UML models executing the created model transformations. The execution order of the set of model transformations is pre-defined by product line architects. To ensure the consistency of the created template instances after the model transformations are executed, the Czarnecki and Antkiewicz's approach proposes two additional processing steps: *patch application* and *simplification*. A patch is a transformation that automatically fixes a problem that may result from removing elements. It is defined for situations in which there exists a unique and intuitive solution to a problem created by element removal. Simplification involves removing elements that have become redundant after removing other elements.

Figure 8.2 [CZA 05] presents an example of a UML class diagram with annotations. In this example, some of the annotations indicate the following: the class Category is present in a template instance if the feature Categories appears in a feature configuration, a containment hierarchy for `Category` is present if the feature `MultiLevel` is selected, the class `Asset` is present in a template instance if the feature `AssociatedAsset` is chosen, the feature `PhysicalGoods` implies the attribute `weight` in the class `Product`, and so on.

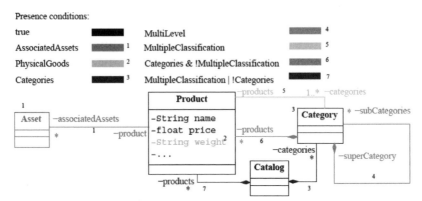

Figure 8.2. *Example of a UML class diagram with annotations [CZA 05] (for a color version of this figure, see www.iste.co.uk/arboleda/SPLeng.zip)*

8.9.2. *The Wagelaar's approach*

Problem space: expressing variability and configuring products. The Wagelaar's approach [WAG 05, WAG 08a, WAG 08b] focuses on variability related to technological platforms. The author proposes an explicit *platform model*, which serves as a vocabulary for describing technological platforms. The platform model is expressed using the Web Ontology Language (OWL) [SMI 04].

Ontologies are commonly used to represent domain knowledge and to provide a controlled vocabulary in specific domains. OWL supports the necessary concepts of a general ontology language, such as *classes, properties, individuals,* and *relationships* between these individuals. In OWL, domain concepts are generally represented as simple named classes, which can have subclasses. Class members or instances are called individuals. Properties allow us to assert general facts about members of classes and specific facts about individuals. A property is a binary relationship. Two types of properties are distinguished, *datatype* and *object* properties. Datatype properties describe relations between instances of classes and primitive data types. Object properties describe relations between instances of two classes.

To capture variation points and variants regarding particular technological platforms, the author creates instances of the platform model, or *platform instances* for short. Each platform instance is composed of a set of class members or OWL individuals of the ontology representing the platform model. Figure 8.3 [WAG 08b] presents an example of a platform instance for describing Java runtime environments. The JavaPackageManager is a class member of the class platform:PackageManager, which is a class from the platform model. This class member or individual represents a variation point with three possible variants, JavaWebApplet, JavaWebStart, and JavaMIDlet. Thus, a product line architect may create different platform instances for different technological platforms.

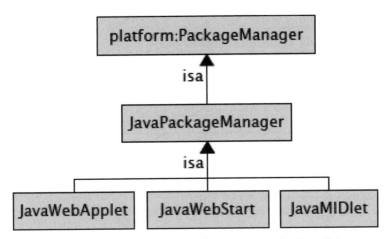

Figure 8.3. *Example of a platform instance for describing Java runtime environments [WAG 08b]*

The author proposes creating *configuration metamodels* as a means to complement the expression of variability taking into account concerns from different technological platforms. Figure 8.4 [WAG 08b] presents a metamodel capturing possible variations of the SPL of an instant messenger. In the figure, the UserInterface metaconcept represents a variation point with three variants, AWTUserInterface, SwingUserInterface, and LCDUIUserInterface. The Packaging metaconcept represents a variation point with three variants, WebAppletPackaging, IpkgPackaging, and MIDletPackaging. The JabberTransport metaconcept represents a variation point with two variants, Default JabberTransport and MEJabberTransport. Therefore, a product designer could, for instance, configure an instant messenger with a SwingUserInterface, while also selecting the WebAppletPackaging as the packaging method and the DefaultJabberTransport as the jabber transporter.

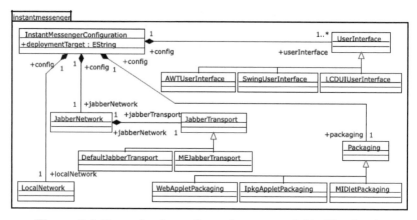

Figure 8.4. *Example of a configuration metamodel in Wagelaar's approach [WAG 08b]*

The approach suggests extending configuration metamodels with annotations based on platform instances. This linking between configuration metamodels and technological platform constraints allows imposing certain technological platform dependencies on the choices provided by the configuration metamodel. Then, products are configured by creating configuration models that conform to configuration metamodels. Thus, whenever a model element is included in a configuration model, the platform dependency constraints (related to its metaconcept) apply.

Solution space: core assets development and products derivation. As in Czarnecki and Antkiewicz's approach, product line members are derived from UML class models created as *templates*. Each template model is created for a group of variants included in a configuration metamodel. A template model represents a superimposition of all the possible classes, properties, and operations required to include their respective variants in a final product. Figure 8.5 [WAG 08b] presents an example of a template model. This template model is created for the JabberTransport variation point from Figure 8.4. Then, a template instance is derived from this template model according to the variant selected for a product designer: DefaultJabberTransport or MEJabberTransport. Some of the class elements, their properties, and operations are annotated. These annotations are used during the process of transforming the template models into final products.

Product line architects create several groups of model transformations to derive products from template models. Each group is in charge of transforming one template model into a part of a final product that runs on a particular technological platform. Thus, when a product designer creates a configuration model and selects a target technological platform, the template models related to the selected variants are transformed using the respective group of model transformations created for the selected target technological platform.

Decision models are not explicitly created to support the product derivation process. The resolution of variability is performed by product designers creating configuration models and selecting a target technological platform. The *effects* on template models, which are used as starting core assets to derive products, are specified in the model transformations. Therefore, the *effects* must be expressed in terms of the model transformations. What model transformations must be used, and the execution ordering required to include selected variants?

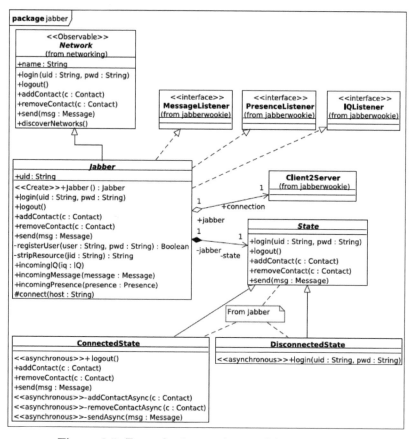

Figure 8.5. *Example of a template model in Wagelaar's approach [WAG 08b]*

The selection of the groups of model transformations to be used is defined from the selected variants, i.e. the model elements included in the configuration models, and the selected target technological platform. The execution ordering of the model transformations is predefined by creating a type of *abstract* execution ordering. The *abstract* execution ordering defines the required sequence of calls to *abstract* transformation rules. The *concrete* transformation rules are executed once the groups of model transformations to be used are defined from the selected variants and the selected target technological platform.

To replace the abstract transformation rules by the concrete transformation rules during execution of the model transformations, the authors propose a composition technique they call *module superimposition*. To apply this technique, transformation rules must be grouped in *modules*. This technique allows the modification of an execution ordering, which includes transformation rules from a module "m-1", overriding it to include: (1) new calls to transformation rules from a module different from "m-1", and (2) calls to transformation rules with the same names and the same parameters that are included in the module "m-1", but from a module different from "m-1". This mechanism has been implemented using the ATLAS Transformation Language (ATL) [JOU 05].

8.9.3. *Loughran et al.'s approach*

In [LOU 08, SAN 08] the authors propose a powerful approach that relies on some feature-oriented models and programming.

Problem space: expressing variability and configuring products. Loughran *et al.* propose an approach where variability is expressed using cardinality-based feature models. Products are configured creating feature configurations.

The main purpose of Loughran *et al.* is to provide support for composition of software *components* based on feature configurations. Configuration of products could be performed by product designers in one or several stages. However, the authors only consider one configuration stage to capture domain (non-architectural) choices.

Solution space: core assets development and products derivation. Product line members are derived from component models of UML 2.0. A set of component models is created for each feature in the feature model. Additionally, a set of common components is created. Common components are present in every product of the product line. Figure 8.6 [SAN 08] presents an example of a feature model (top) and a reference architecture model (bottom) including the set of components related to the different features. Thus, for example, if the `Keypad` feature is selected in a feature configuration, the `KeypadReader` component must be connected to the common component `LockControlMng` to derive a final product.

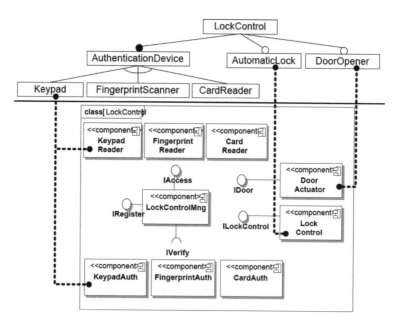

Figure 8.6. *Example of reference architecture in Loughran et al.'s approach [SAN 08]*

Loughran *et al.* propose a language – *VML*, to express how software components must be composed according to feature configurations. VML includes constructs that correspond to possible operations on components such as *connect (component-1, component-2)* or *disconnect(component-1, component-2)*. VML also supports the specification of links between features and components, indicating how the components of the reference architecture model must be composed according to features selected in feature configurations. For example, it is possible to specify that the KeypadReader component must be connected to the common component LockControlMng using the interface IAccess if the Keypad feature was selected in a feature configuration. Listing 8.1 presents the VML specification for this example.

```
1   Concern  LockControl {
2     VariationPoint  AuthenticationDevice {
3     Kind:  alternative ;
4       Variant  Keypad {
5     SELECT:
6         connect ( KeypadReader , LockControlMng )
7           using  interface ( IAccess );
8     UNSELECT:
9         remove ( KeypadReader );
10  }
```

Listing 8.1. *Example of a VML specification*

Therefore, VML allows for creating decision models using its well-structured constructs. Using the VML constructs, it is possible to relate (1) a set of *effects* on the reference architecture and (2) features in a determinate state (selected/unselected). For instance, from Listing 8.1, if the *Keypad* feature is SELECTED then VML executes commands from lines 6 and 7 else the *Keypad* feature is UNSELECTED and then VML executes commands from line 9. Commands from lines 6, 7 and 9 imply *effects* on the reference architecture. Using the VML constructs, it is not possible, however, to relate (1) a set of *effects* on the reference architecture model and (2) a subset of features in determinate states. For instance, it is not possible to have both the *Keypad* feature SELECTED, the *CardReader* feature UNSELECTED and to execute a set of commands.

To transform VML specifications into a set of model transformations in charge of transforming reference architecture models into final products, the authors have created a High Order Transformation (HOT). A HOT is a model transformation that generates other model transformations. For executing the created HOT, the authors propose first to transform VML specifications into models that conform to a *VML metamodel*. Thus, for instance, for line 6 of the VML specification from Listing 8.1, the HOT generates a transformation rule to transform the reference architecture model from Figure 8.6 into a model including the connection between the KeypadReader and LockControlMng components by using the IAccess interface.

Thus, when a product designer creates a feature configuration, the generated model transformations are executed and the final product is derived. The execution ordering of the generated model transformations must be predefined, and they are fixed to avoid inconsistencies in the final product.

8.9.4. *Voelter and Groher's approach*

Voelter and Groher, in [VÖL 07b], provide a tool chain, which inspired our work.

Problem space: expressing variability and configuring products. Voelter and Groher's approach proposes to create metamodels in conjunction with *cardinality-based* feature models to capture and express variability. This approach supports the explicit and separated modeling of variability in metamodels and feature models. Product line architects create different metamodels during domain engineering; each metamodel captures some concerns related to different points of view. One metamodel is the *domain metamodel*, which serves as a standard vocabulary to practitioners of the system's domain. A domain model does not include concepts regarding details of the structure or processing of the system. Other metamodels are the *architectural metamodel*, which contains software architectural concerns, and the *platform metamodel*, which contains technological platform concerns.

Only one feature model is created grouping different concerns. This approach is particularly concerned with staged-configuration and staged-derivation of products. To configure a product, first a product designer creates a model that conforms to the domain metamodel. Then, another product designer selects features from the feature model including choices from concerns that are different from the general application domain.

Solution space: core assets development and products derivation. Products are derived from (1) domain models, (2) re-usable models that conform to the architectural and platform metamodels, (3) re-usable pieces of source code, and (4) model transformations in charge of adapting the re-usable models, and pieces of code according to domain models and the valid feature configurations.

For each feature in the feature model, the authors suggest the creation of a set of re-usable models, source code, and model transformations. Model transformations are created to transform (1) domain models into architectural models, (2) architectural models into platform models, and finally, (3) platform models into source code. Thus, if a feature is selected in a feature configuration, the domain model is incrementally transformed using the model transformations associated with the selected feature. The model transformations not only create new model structures in the architectural and platform domains, but they also take the re-usable models and weave them into the newly created model structures. Similarly, in the latest transformation, the model-to-text transformations create source code and re-use pieces of code to build final products.

For the implementation of this approach, the authors use the oAW framework, including its AOP mechanism (see section 3.6.4). Thus, decision models are created as oAW workflows, textual descriptors, to support the product derivation process. In these descriptors, the authors indicate the model transformations that must be executed and the required execution ordering according to selected features. For modifying the execution ordering coping with feature configurations, the authors have created a new oAW component. This component allows for querying a feature configuration at model transformation execution time, and weaving an oAW aspect if a particular feature appears in the configuration (selected or unselected).

```
1
2  <feature isSelected="featureExample">
3    <transformationAspect adviceTarget="baseModelTransformation">
4      <extensionAdvice value="transformationAdvice"/>
5    </transformationAspect>
6  </feature>
7
8  <transform id="baseModelTransformation">
9    <invoke value="transformationRuleBase(domainModel)"/>
10   <outputSlot value="architectureModel"/>
11 </transform>
```

Listing 8.2. *Example of a workflow using the Voelter and Groher's component*

Listing 8.2 presents an example of an oAW workflow by using the created component. The `baseModel Transformation` from line 6 transforms a domain model into an architectural model. For this, the first rule to be executed is `transformationRuleBase(domainModel)` (line 9). The normal call graph of this rule is modified if the `featureExample` is selected. This is specified in line 2. If the feature appears selected in a feature configuration, the `transformationAdvice` is executed, thus modifying the base execution ordering. For details of how the AOP mechanism of oAW works see section 3.6.4 and [OAW 09].

8.9.5. *Comparison table*

Table 8.1 presents a comparison summary based on the discussion presented in this section.

	Czarnecki and Antkiewicz	Wagelaar	Loughran *et al.*	Voelter and Groher
Metamodeling for expressing variability and modeling for configuring products	No	Yes	No	Yes
Multi-staged configuration of products	No	No	No	Yes
Expression of *fine-grained* variations and creation of *fine-grained* configurations	No	No	No	No
Creation of explicit decision models	No	No	Yes	Yes
Decision models take into account the effects that possible feature combinations may have in final products	n/a	n/a	No	Yes
Decision models are independent of particular implementation languages	n/a	n/a	Yes	No
Selection of transformation rules according to selected variants	No	Yes	Yes	Yes
Modification of transformation rules' execution ordering according to selected variants	No	Yes	No	Yes
Mechanisms for modifying execution ordering of transformation rules independent of particular model transformation languages	n/a	No	n/a	Yes

Table 8.1. *Related work's comparison table*

8.10. Dynamic variability

The notion of dynamic variability has different meanings. The first general meaning is related to the binding time of variants to variation points that can ultimately occur at runtime. For instance, it is used in context-aware and adaptive systems, which need automatic adaptation to changes in their environment. In this case, the management of changes in variability due to modifications in requirements or software evolution in general, is the main concern. Techniques such as reflexivity, late binding, and conditions can be used here. This dynamic variability is required for software adaptive systems, service robotics, ubiquitous systems, and medical devices. Dynamic software product lines [HAL 08] are mainly concerned with binding variation points at runtime; thus, they rely on dynamic variability. Two recent illustrations of researches on dynamic variability are: Context awareness product lines of [PAR 09] and the DIVA project[2]. A presentation of the DIVA approach can be found in Chapter 12 of the AMPLE book [RAS 11]. Dynamic software product lines, as defined in [PAR 09], are product lines devoted to generate products reacting to changes in their environment. This goal implies reconsidering the development process of product lines and using recent techniques, such as MDE, AOP, AOM, context awareness, and adaptation. Even if evolution and adaptation arise at different times in the development process, it seems suitable to unify them. The proposal, called CAPucine, for Context Aware Software Product Line, adds a runtime derivation process to the classic SPL engineering process. The design derivation process is controlled by the developer team while the runtime one is automatically managed by the events denoting changes in the execution context. The set of core assets is enriched with aspect models, which correspond to alternatives and options of the features models and can be woven at design time or at runtime. An aspect model

---

2 http://www.ict-diva.eu/.

captures a variant and is compounded by an event, a model, an advice, and a pointcut. This concept unifies the assets for design and runtime and proposes a simple but general model to establish a straight link between feature model, architecture, and implementation. The concept of aspect model is described by metamodel and specific languages devoted to expression of pointcuts and events that have been designed. The runtime derivation needs a specific lifecycle based on an adaptation loop that involves acquiring change events, deciding and validating the reconfiguration, and then processing the chosen reconfiguration.

A second more narrow meaning is related to the specification of dynamic behavior in a product line. In a specification, several plans or views can be distinguished. Often, the specification is reduced to structural and functional aspects while dynamic behavior is forgotten. Dynamic behavior expresses the control, the communication, and the concurrency constraints between the entities in the specification. This behavior adds some important information to the specification and paves the way to more advanced verifications such as model-checking. This is a current situation with UML, where use cases and static diagrams are the main pieces; sometimes, message sequence charts are used but rarely state charts. Most of the MD-SPL approaches do not deal with full dynamic behavior. At least two main problems arise. The first one is to elaborate dynamic diagrams and to get the complete specification. The second one is to integrate this dynamic behavior into the production plan until code generation. However, there are some attempts to overcome this deficiency. One approach for this is given by Ziadi and Jézéquel in [ZIA 06]. The principle is to use message sequence charts to build the state charts since one message chart denotes the cooperation of several state charts. It does not solve all the above problems but helps in constructing state charts, which can be improved later by the designer. In [GOM 04] a different way is proposed. The dynamic variability is described as logical expressions used to parameterize the state charts. In some sense, it enables the configuration of the dynamic behavior according to the features selected in a product. There is a need to improve MD-SPL to address dynamic variability; one new aspect is the existence of international workshops dedicated to this issue.

8.11. Domain specific languages

A domain specific language (DSL) is a language devoted to a specific area of expertise; it is a language tailored for particular application contexts. In DSLs, the language concepts represent things in the domain context, not the code context. The language follows the domain semantics and abstractions, allowing developers to perceive themselves as working directly with domain concepts. DSLs can be seen as opposed to general purpose languages such as C++ or Java, which can express any domain and any computation on these domains. The rules of the domain can be included in the language as constructs or constraints, ideally making it impossible to specify illegal programs. The close alignment of DSLs and domain problems offer several benefits. Many of these benefits are common to other strategies for moving toward higher levels of abstraction: better system quality, better tackling of complexity, and improved productivity. Every domain contains its own specific concepts, constructs, and semantics. Therefore, DSLs need to be specific for each domain. Domain concepts are more natural and reflect the underlying computational models, which are typically already known and in use, and needed to design the products. Final code can still be generated from these high-level specifications. The main principle for the automated code generation from DSLs is that both the generators and languages have to fit the selected context requirements.

This is a current active area of research; it was identified as an important technology for generative programming in [CZA 02]. DSLs cover a wide variety of forms and techniques [MER 05, CZA 02]; the interested reader should refer to more specific literature. There are several important benefits of defining and creating DSLs:

– They are specific to a domain; thus, they may be used to interact with stakeholders or clients, who are definitely not designers or programmers. For instance, requirements elicitation, spreadsheet computation, resources or energy consumption are examples of domains where DSLs already exist.

– They are not designed to express every concept of the world; thus, the re-use of programs written with DSLs is simpler and safer than with general purpose languages.

– They are more restricted; some properties related to the domain can be easily expressed and enforced.

A simple and well-known example is the BNF language for grammar descriptions. Another example is a DSL for defining type systems of programming languages, which includes type checking. By means of such languages, types can be easily defined and type checking rules can be written. In the context of SPLE, there is a need for various DSLs. On the one hand there are those related to capturing development artifacts, such as requirements or use cases (see a proposal in [RAS 11]). On the other hand there are those specific to domains where SPLs are created; e.g. automotive industry, ERP systems, etc.

Generally, a language is defined through its grammar and semantics [MER 05]. Recently, the use of MDE emerged as an effective means to define DSLs by means of models; these are Domain-Specific Modeling Languages. A metamodel defines an abstract grammar and syntactic constraints; thus, it can easily represent a DSL. MDE frameworks provide tools to support the concrete syntax creation and various related activities. Thus, Domain-Specific Modeling can be seen as the definition of languages, editors, and generators for particular domains by means of models. One result of the activities around DSLs, MDE, and DSM is the raising of *software language engineering* as a new research domain.

8.12. Additional references

Finally, we mention the main events related to model-driven and product line engineering. During the Third Software Product Line Conference (SPLC 2004), the steering committee decided to merge the SPLC with its European counterpart, the Product Family Engineering (PFE) conference. With the 9th International Software Product Line Conference (SPLC-Europe 2005) [SPL 11], this new organization was inaugurated. Since then, this is the most important event bringing together MD-SPLs, practitioners, and researchers. The 11th Conference on Generative Programming and Component Engineering (GPCE) [GPC 11] took place in 2011. This conference brought together people interested in techniques that used program generation and component deployment to increase productivity. The International Conference on Model-Driven Engineering Languages and Systems (MODELS) [MOD 11] was the space for the exchange of innovative ideas and experiences of model-based approaches in the development of complex systems. The International Workshop on Model-Driven Approaches in Software Product Line Engineering (MAPLE) [MAP 11] and the International Workshop on Model-Driven Product Line Engineering (MDPLE) [MDP 11] are equivalent events in conjunction with SPLC and the European Conference on Model-Driven Architecture (ECMDA) [ECM 11].

The special CACM issue for software product lines [CAC 06] is a useful piece of information since it provides several survey articles written by well-known specialists. The guest editors [SUG 06] give some information about SPLE and its history. Clements *et al.* in [CLE 06] discuss how the Adoption Factory pattern helps. Product line adoption requires the mapping of the technical and business activities in a consistent way. In [KRU 06], C. Kruger examines the next-generation methods for SPL. Pohl and Metzger wrote a short article with the main references and challenges related to testing. Software product line testing [POH 06a] is a problem not addressed in recent work. Verification and validation of requirements engineering is important to increase reliability and adequacy of software systems.

Feature model verification and validation is a recent and active area of research; several directions are successful and important progress has been made in this context. As it concerns mainly requirements, early verification and validation solutions are preferable. Requirement reviews or natural language analysis can be used to validate feature models. As already said, the AMPLE approach [RAS 11] suggests a way to analyze, organize, and extract a feature model for requirements in natural languages. This provides a valuable tool and an approach allowing validation from the stakeholders.

One survey about the analyses of feature models is [BEN 06]. Obviously, the verification of feature models depends on the complexity of the notations; for instance, cardinality, constraint, or group concepts introduces more difficulties. Verification of feature models is an issue explored by several researchers, mainly using constraint programming, description logic, BDD, and satisfiability techniques. In [BAT 06], the authors present some of the main challenges. Of course we need automatic and efficient techniques. General properties such as completeness or consistency can be formulated and sometimes proved over formally specified systems. Techniques such as formal proofs or model-checking can be used as soon as the system is formally specified. As the feature model is close to propositional or first-order logic, several attempts were made to use formal declarative languages or OCL and associated tools.

Czarnecki and Pietroszek [CZA 06] propose to analyze feature-based model templates, that is, a feature model and an annotated UML model describing additional semantics of the feature model. They use a translation into OCL expressions of the template model and a SAT solver to automatically check that configured instances are compliant with the template's feature model. Since the number of systems represented by a feature model is large, two issues are the scalability of modeling and the efficiency of verification. In [CLA 10] the authors address these issues by defining the notion of the featured transition system and then using the model-checking technique to check properties on the model.

8.13. Summary

There are several books focusing on software product line engineering. The most relevant, from our point of view, are Northop and Clements' book and Pohl, Böckle and Vander Linden's book. There are also extensions of UML. Gommaa's book provides a practical and seamless approach in this context. However, product line engineering needs more sophisticated techniques and more advanced languages. The AMPLE Book is a recent book covering most of the engineering processes and uses modern techniques such as variability languages, MDE, AOP, natural processing language, etc. Our current book is focused on the use of model-driven engineering for a product line. It covers the overall design, the derivation tool chain, variability management with multiple stages, and fine-grained variability. There are many topics only overviewed here requiring more detail. Dynamic variability, domain-specific languages, and decision models are some of them. They will be more important in the future of MD-SPL engineering.

Chapter 9

Conclusion

The intent of this book is threefold. First, it is a pedagogical tool for undergraduate and graduate students to understand what a product line is and why it is so important in modern software engineering. Second, the technical parts are dedicated to engineers who want to launch a software product line chain using model engineering. Both product lines and model-driven engineering are becoming popular techniques for software development. Finally, this book also "tags" some challenges, some open problems, and related work that are of interest for software researchers. Due to the complexity of SPL, this is an area where various techniques and theories are interacting and growing. For instance, there is research about requirements engineering, natural language processing, and construction of feature models. A feature model can be seen as a new logic formalism for organizing requirements and advanced verification techniques; proof-based or model-checking are needed. There is an important requirement to define languages for variability at various stages of the development cycle. Defining reference architecture is a complex task and automating the production chain is far from completion. Implementation languages could benefit from better variability mechanisms, and there is an opportunity to enrich or extend existing programming languages to cope with variability and to close the gap from variability to source code.

The next section summarizes the main concepts and notations introduced in this book. Then, the last section outlines some issues of MD-SPL engineering discussed in the previous chapters and concludes with some perspectives.

9.1. Book summary

One can observe that many software companies are building applications that share more commonalities than differences. They often repeatedly add new features and build new variants or releases of their applications. The strategy of systematic and planned re-use of software artifacts was seen as a means to improve software cost, productivity, and quality. Software product line engineering is a new trend in software development, which promotes the re-usability of artifacts. Benefits of a product line are clear, provided that the initial investment has been precisely measured. Engineers do not have to minimize the complexity and the organization needed to successfully launch and manage a software product line. This engineering involves a complex two-fold software development process: domain engineering and application engineering. Domain engineering is responsible for defining the domain scope and modeling the variability of the product line. This is an important and critical engineering step where the core assets are built and the production plan to derive products is made. The variability model is a structured representation of the commonalities and the variabilities of the products in the scope of the line. Abstractly, a variability model is a base description with variation points and their associated variants. One of the main notations is feature modeling; however, metamodels are increasingly used to represent variability. Application engineering is the process of creating a product from the product configuration and the core assets following the production plan. The product configuration is an assembly of variants binding the variation points defined in the variability model. There are still numerous issues in SPLE: Variability management, product derivation, core assets exploitation, testing, traceability and tool support are some of these.

Model-driven engineering is another new trend in software engineering. It considers that models and transformations are governing software development. Thus, the whole software development cycle is viewed as a process of creation, iterative refinement, and integration of models. Models are first-class entities that denote a viewpoint of a system. Each model conforms to a metamodel making the grammar and the constraints of a particular concern explicit. Domain-specific modeling is used to develop software systems, and it involves the use of a domain-specific modeling language to represent the different concerns of an application domain. Model transformations appear to be one of the most important operations on models. They are software artifacts that implement algorithms to transform models that conform to source metamodels into models that conform to target metamodels. Transformations are often classified as model-to-model, model-to-text, or text-to-model transformations. Transformations can use a declarative or an imperative style; in the latter, we express the transformation scheduling. Vertical transformations are model transformations crosscutting the level of abstractions. Horizontal transformations are mechanisms to transform models at the same level of abstraction but integrating several concerns or points of view of an application domain. MDE technologies are now mature technologies and tool supports such as the Eclipse modeling framework, the Topcased toolkit, and the oAW framework. Model transformation languages exist as QVT, ATL, or the Xtend and Xpand from oAW.

MDE appears as an effective technique for product lines since it provides uniformity and abstraction for software artifacts and processes. The ability to build complex transformations is crucial to automate domain and application engineering. Model-driven engineering techniques and tools have the potential to increase the productivity and quality of software engineering processes significantly. The integration of both approaches requires a tight coupling and tuning of the derivation chain. To develop complex and modern systems, we can use several points of view, which can be captured in different models. This implies capturing the variability in different models conforming to metamodels, configuring the product, and defining an automated production chain relying on a multi-staged process. Examples of variability models are feature models that organize the client requirements whereas architectural models are concerned with the structure of software. The derivation process is a complex task, and it requires sequences of transformations with a precise scheduling. Decision models are artifacts specifying base and specific transformation rules for scheduling the rules for both commonality and variability. Decision models capture transformational aspects of the baseline derivation process to derive specific variable applications.

This general MD-SPL process is effective, but it is not always flexible enough for fine-grained configuration. We have to go further to configure differently several instances of the same kind of artifacts. The purpose of the FieSta approach is to extend MD-SPL processes to cope with fine-grained variation and configuration. The fine-grained variation arises when we need to define variable artifacts of the same kind. Coarse-grained approaches do not allow the configuration of different instances of the same metamodel. To solve this issue, the concepts of binding and constraint models are introduced. Binding models allow the capture of the links between a model and a variability model, thus, enabling the fine-grained configuration of model elements. On the other hand, the constraint model specifies precisely the semantics of the bindings using cardinality and structural dependency properties. Metamodels were created to support the creation of constraint, binding, and decision models. The baseline scheduling of the rules is modified according to valid feature configurations and bindings of the binding models. Aspects, which are responsible for the scheduling of rules associated with variations query the binding model to get the precise element impacted by the rule. The decision metamodel has been extended to allow for deriving products taking into account binding models.

A set of plug-ins has been defined to support the metamodels required by the FieSta approach. The approach and the tools are illustrated in two case studies. The first one, the smart home system, is a classic in product line engineering. The second one is typical of many business applications where variations are important for presentation, persistence, or interoperability, but where computation and control are quite simple or standard. This is a simple stand-alone, yet generic, application managing data collection.

9.2. MD-SPL engineering

Today, software engineers need to be aware about modern development techniques such as the ones discussed in this book. As summarized in the previous section, there are important advantages of using SPL and MDE; however, the total amount of benefits is greater than the sum of its parts. Nevertheless, this engineering is complex and tricky. The first step is to acquire the SPL and MDE principles and to merge them both in a consistent and efficient way. The general process presented in Chapter 4 is a compound from metamodels and models to capture domain scope and product configuration. Transformation rules and decision models are used to automate the production plan. We analyze some related issues: multiple points of view, multiple variability models, and multi-stage processes to model variation, to configure and to generate the products. This first level does not allow fine-grained variations and configurations.

The second level is to introduce a way to take into account specific features at the level of metamodel instances. This obviously complicates the modeling and the derivation tool chain.

The FieSta approach is our MD-SPL chain coping with fine-grained variations and configurations. In this section, we analyze the advantages and drawbacks of FieSta regarding the MD-SPL engineering mechanisms. We focus on two aspects impacted by fine-grained variability: i) variability expression and product configuration in MD-SPL, and ii) the derivation of configured products. We also compare FieSta with other MD-SPL approaches.

9.2.1. *Metamodeling and feature modeling*

We use metamodeling and feature modeling for capturing and expressing variability. Metamodels facilitate modeling variations at the language level. Product designers, for instance, building architects, are capable of configuring different products by creating diverse building models. Feature modeling allows us to configure products by selecting features. Therefore, for instance, facilities designers and software architects can configure products without the need for creating complex models.

Using feature modeling and metamodeling separately gives us the flexibility and power of expression of metamodels, and the simplicity of feature models. We have also proposed to relate metamodels and feature models to create what we have named constraint models. Constraint models allow us to express fine-grained variations between products of MD-SPL. We have shown how to express the possible fine-grained variations between products of an MD-SPL by creating relationships between metamodels and feature models. For example, fine-grained variations allow us to express that two Smart-Home systems could be different in the location of their automatic windows.

As we demonstrated in Chapter 6 and in [ARB 09], our mechanism for expressing fine-grained variations between products of an MD-SPL by using constraint models extends the expressive power of variability in MD-SPL, and consequently, extends the scope of products that can be fine-grained configured.

9.2.2. *Multi-staged configuration of products*

Our approach supports the modeling of variability in several stages. We allow product line architects, at different (staged) times, to express and capture coarse and fine-grained variations between members of product lines. This helps product line architects with different skills to focus on particular concerns at different times.

At configuration time, we allow product designers configuring products at different binding times to choose at each stage specific variants to create domain models and binding models. Thus, we postponed the binding time of variations facilitating the intervention of stakeholders with different profiles in the configuration process. For instance, facilities designers and software architects can provide their choices for the facilities and software architecture of Smart-Homes, at different times.

9.2.3. *Coarse and fine-grained variations and configurations*

As far as we know, our approach is the only MD-SPL approach allowing the creation of fine-grained configurations and derivation of products based on such configurations. This adds expressive power to variability modeling, which usually only captures coarse-grained variability. We have presented the way to model fine-grained configurations between product line members by means of binding models. A binding model allows us to configure model elements individually based on features. For example, we have created a binding to indicate that the feature Periodic Component affects individually the component Air Conditioning Controller, and the feature Keypad affects individually the door mainDoorD2. We first introduced our mechanism for creating fine-grained configurations in [GAR 07], then we used it in [ARB 07a, ARB 07b, ANQ 08, ARB 09].

9.2.4. *Core assets development and decision models*

We improved the use of explicit decision models in MD-SPL engineering. Our decision models allow us to capture separately i) the base and specific model transformation rules used to derive product line members, ii) the variants represented in feature models, and iii) the relationships between model transformations and variants. Decision models are the key of our mechanism to compose model transformations and adapt their execution ordering according to particular product configurations.

Other approaches such as Loughran *et al.*'s approach [LOU 08, SAN 08] and Voelter and Groher's approach [VÖL 07b] have proposed the use of decision models. Our approach, however, is concerned with both the problem of transformation rules composition based on product configurations, which is a complex problem in MD-SPL engineering, and the independence from model transformation languages to create decision models. As we have presented before in section 8.9, the Loughran *et al.* approach is only concerned with the composition of software components, and the Voelter and Groher's approach is restricted to the use of a platform-dependent language, Xtend, to create decision models. Furthermore, our mechanism based on decision models to derive products takes into account that several features selected together may imply different adaptations than those required when features are selected separately. This is not taken into account by the Loughran *et al.* approach. Our decision models also capture the required information about how transformation rules must be composed to derive fine-grained configured products. Given that our approach takes into account fine-grained variations and fine-grained configurations, it also copes with the derivation of fine-grained configured products. Our decision models have been presented in [ARB 09a, ARB 09b, ARB 08].

9.2.5. *Product derivation*

Based on our decision models, we propose a mechanism for selecting transformation rules and modifying their execution ordering according to selected variants. In our current implementation, we have used the model transformation engine of oAW to execute model transformation workflows derived from our decision models. Our decision models, however, are independent of model transformation languages and can be used to support product derivation in contexts different from the oAW context. For instance, currently, we explore how our decision models can be used to derive products by using the ATL language and its facilities for transformation rules composition [ROM 09]. Further work on this field is part of our future work. Our mechanism for product derivation has been presented in [ARB 09a, ARB 08].

9.2.6. *Comparison table*

Table 9.1 presents a summary of this section taking into account our approach and the related approaches. This table summarizes the comparaison of MD-SPL approaches (the rows). The lines represent the various characteristics we previously discussed (yes/no meaning presence/absence and n/a for not applicable).

We believe that our MDE mechanisms are scalable to traditional SPL engineering where models are used only as artifacts for documentation. Currently, MDE is being used not only in academia but also in industry. Several international events, journals, and research projects are concerned about the

	FieSta	Czarnecki and Antkiewicz	Wagelaar	Loughran *et al.*	Voelter and Groher
Metamodeling for expressing variability and modeling for configuring products	Yes	No	Yes	No	Yes
Multi-staged configuration of products	Yes	No	No	No	Yes
Expression of *fine-grained* variations and creation of *fine-grained* configurations	Yes	No	No	No	No
Creation of explicit decision models	Yes	No	No	Yes	Yes
Decision models take into account the effects that possible feature combinations may have in final products	Yes	n/a	n/a	No	Yes
Decision models independent of particular implementation languages	Yes	n/a	n/a	Yes	No
Selection of transformation rules according to selected variants	Yes	No	Yes	Yes	Yes
Mechanisms to modify the rules execution ordering according to selected variants	Yes	No	Yes	No	Yes
Mechanisms for modifying execution ordering of transformation rules independent of particular model transformation languages	Yes	n/a	No	n/a	Yes

Table 9.1. *Summary of the discussion regarding our contribution to the MD-SPL engineering domain*

subject. Thus, a body of knowledge including tool support is being created to support MDE. We have shown through this book how our MDE mechanisms contribute toward making SPL engineering more feasible and profitable, and consequently more interesting for SPL developers to adopt it.

9.2.7. *Perspectives*

In this book, we integrated model-driven engineering and software product line engineering. The following subsection presents some continuation of this work.

We discussed in section 5.4 some limitations of our approach. We consider it important to improve our approach overcoming such limitations. First, a mechanism is required to validate that for each possible feature configuration, product line architects provide the required transformation rules to derive valid products. Second, another mechanism is required that allows product line architects to capture possible feature interactions by means of scenarios, and thus, to create and relate transformation rules to such scenarios. Finally, it is required to consider bindings that satisfy several constraints when execution ordering of transformation rules is modified according to binding models.

We focused on the use of feature models as variability models. However, other variability models, such as ontology models or the one presented by Bayer *et al.* [BAY 06], involve other relevant concepts differencing only in Group, Grouped or Solitary Feature. These variability models deserve special attention for the rich semantics they provide to express variability in product lines. We consider it fruitful to integrate ontology models into our approach to complement feature models, to improve the expressive power of variability models, and to extend the scope of MD-SPL.

Our approach supports staged capture of variability, and also staged configuration of products. We showed, using our case study, how one of these stages involved concerns about software architecture based on components. For this, we created one specialized metamodel capturing concepts of component-based software development. There are, however, several Architectural Description Languages (ADL) such as [ASI 07, DAS 05, RAS 11], which are based on metamodels that include very complete information about architectural concerns. We consider it important to include the use of these ADLs into our approach to extend the scope of variations we are able to manage regarding software architecture, irrespective of the domain of the MD-SPL we are interested in developing.

We considered AOP as a suitable paradigm to tackle the problem of adapting the execution ordering of transformation rules. Recent work (see [ASP 08]), has shown how AOM is a valuable paradigm to be incorporated in model-driven engineering. AOM allows product line architects to create re-usable models, which during the derivation of product line members can be woven with other models according to variability choices performed by product designers. We believe that AOM enables the explicit expression and modularization of variability on model level and facilitates the maintainability and re-use of models as core assets. Thus, we consider it important to integrate AOM in our approach.

Declarative programming minimizes side effects by describing *what* the program should accomplish, rather than describing *how* to go about accomplishing it [LLO 94]. Declarative programming in MDE has a number of advantages. Declarative transformation rules are based on specifying relations between source and target patterns, hiding the details related to selection of source elements, rule triggering, and ordering [JOU 05]. We believe that the integration of declarative transformation rules may help to deal with the problem of adapting the execution ordering of transformation rules, given different product configurations.

Furthermore, we currently explore constraint programming, which is a type of declarative programming, to tackle the problem of relating transformation rules to sets of variants with particular interactions stated in the form of constraints. The idea of using constraints to define suitable configurations can be extended to the design and implementation of a constraint system specialized in those kind of constraints, in which all the power of specialized solvers can be used to validate configurations. Likewise, it could be important to explore if modeling the transformation of the problem of scheduling rules using constraints can be a more efficient way to solve it, instead of using aspect-oriented programming.

We have started a study tending to formalize our approach using basic set theory. Our aim is to generalize our MD-SPL approach making it extensible and independent of specific platform modeling frameworks and/or model transformation languages. One benefit, maybe the most important of such activity, is to get a better insight into product lines and model-driven engineering.

Bibliography

[AMP 08] AMPLE, *Aspect-oriented, Model-driven Product Line Engineering*, www.project-ample.net, 2008.

[ANQ 08] ANQUETIL N., GRAMMEL B., GALVAO I., NOPPEN J., KHAN S.S., ARBOLEDA H., RASHID A., GARCIA A., "Traceability for model driven, software product line engineering", *Proceedings of the 4th Workshop on Traceability of the 4th European Conference on Model Driven Architecture (ECMDA '08)*, Berlin, Germany, June 2008.

[ANQ 09] ANQUETIL N., KULESZA U., MITSCHKE R., MOREIRA A., ROYER J.C., RUMMLER A., SOUSA A., "A model-driven traceability framework for software product lines", *Software and Systems Modeling*, http://www.springerlink.com/content/wvm4hv8r78117785/, 2009.

[ANT 04] ANTKIEWICZ M., CZARNECKI K., "Featureplugin: feature modeling plug-in for eclipse", *Proceedings of the Workshop on Eclipse Technology Exchange of OOPSLA '04*, p. 67-72, 2004.

[ARB 07a] ARBOLEDA H., CASALLAS R., ROYER J.-C., "Dealing with constraints during a feature configuration process in a model-driven software product line", *Proceedings of the 7th Workshop on Domain-Specific Modeling of the 22th ACM Conference on Object-Oriented Programming, Systems, Languages, and Applications (OOPSLA '07)*, p. 178-183, Montreal, Canada, 2007.

[ARB 07b] ARBOLEDA H., CASSALLAS R., ROYER J.-C., "Implementing an MDA approach for managing variability in product line construction using the GMF and GME frameworks", *Proceedings of the 5th Nordic Workshop on Model Driven Software Engineering (NW-MoDE '07)*, p. 67-82, Ronneby, Sweden, August 2007.

[ARB 08] ARBOLEDA H., CASALLAS R., ROYER J.-C., "Using transformation-aspects in model-driven software product lines", *Proceedings of the 3rd International Workshop on Aspects, Dependencies, and Interactions of 22nd European Conference on Object-Oriented Programming (ECOOP '08)*, p. 46-56, Paphos, Cyprus, July 2008.

[ARB 09a] ARBOLEDA H., ROMERO A., CASALLAS R., ROYER J.-C., "Product derivation in a model-driven software product line using decision models", *Proceedings of the 12th Iberoamerican Conference on Requirements Engineering and Software Environments (IDEAS '09)*, p. 59-72, Medellin, Colombia, April 2009.

[ARB 09b] ARBOLEDA H., CASALLAS R., ROYER J.-C., "Dealing with fine-grained configurations in model-driven SPLS", *Proceedings of the 13th International Software Product Line Conference (SPLC '09)*, San Francisco, USA, August 2009.

[ARB 10] ARBOLEDA H., DIAZ J.F., VARGAS V., ROYER J.-C., "Automated reasoning for derivation of model-driven SPLs", DHUNGANA D., GROHER I., RABISER R., THIEL S. (eds), *Proceedings of the 14th International Software Product Line Conference (SPLC 2010), Vol. 2, 2nd International Workshop on Model-driven Approaches in Software Product Line Engineering (MAPLE 2010)*, p. 181-188, Lancaster University, United Kingdom, September 2010.

[ARB 12] ARBOLEDA H., *Model-Driven Software Product Line Engineering: Tool Support and Case Studies*, http://www.icesi.edu.co/i2t/driso/mdsplbook, 2012.

[ASI 07] ASIKAINEN T., MÄNNISTÖ T., SOININEN T., "Kumbang: a domain ontology for modelling variability in software product families", *Advanced Engineering Informatics*, vol. 21, no. 1, p. 23-40, 2007.

[ASP 08] Aspect-oriented modelling workshops website, http://www.aspect-modeling.org/, 2008.

[ATK 00] ATKINSON C., BAYER J., MUTHIG D., "Component-based product line development: the kobra approach", DONOHOE P. (ed.), *Proceedings of 1st Software Product Line Conference*, p. 289-309, Kluwer Academic Publishers, Norwell, MA, USA, 2000.

[BAC 03] BACHMANN F., GOEDICKE M., JULIO, NORD R.L., POHL K., RAMESH B., VILBIG A., "A meta-model for representing variability in product family development", *Proceedings of the 5th International Workshop on Software Product-Family Engineering, Lecture Notes in Computer Science*, vol. 3014, p. 66-80, Springer, Siena, Italy, November 2003.

[BAT 06] BATORY D., BENAVIDES D., RUIZ-CORTES A., "Automated analysis of feature models: challenges ahead", *Communications of the ACM*, vol. 49, no. 12, p. 45-47, December 2006.

[BAY 99] BAYER J., FLEGE O., KNAUBER P., LAQUA R., MUTHIG D., SCHMID K., WIDEN T., DEBAUD J.-M., "Pulse: a methodology to develop software product lines", *Proceedings of the 5th Symposium on Software Reusability (SSR)*, p. 122-131, Los Angeles (California, USA), May 1999.

[BAY 00] BAYER J., FLEGE O., GACEK C., "Creating product line architectures", *IW-SAPF-3: Proceedings of the International Workshop on Software Architectures for Product Families*, p. 210-216, Springer-Verlag, London, UK, 2000.

[BAY 06] BAYER J., GERARD S., HAUGEN Ø., MANSELL J.X., MØLLER-PEDERSEN B., OLDEVIK J., TESSIER P., THIBAULT J.-P., WIDEN T., "Consolidated product line variability modeling", KÄKÖLÄ T., DUEÑAS J.C. (eds), *Software Product Lines - Research Issues in Engineering and Management*, p. 195-241, Springer, 2006.

[BEN 06] BENAVIDES D., RUIZ-CORTÉS A., TRINIDAD P., SEGURA S., "A survey on the automated analyses of feature models", RIQUELME SANTOS J.C., BOTELLA P. (eds), *JISBD*, p. 367-376, 2006.

[BÉZ 05] BÉZIVIN J., "On the unification power of models", *Software and Systems Modeling*, vol. 4, no. 2, p. 171-188, May 2005.

[BOS 00] BOSCH J., *Design and Use of Software Architectures: Adapting and Evolving a Product-Line Approach*, Addison-Wesley, Boston, MA, USA, 2000.

[BOS 02] BOSCH J., FLORIJN G., GREEFHORST D., KUUSELA J., OBBINK H.J., POHL K., "Variability issues in software product lines", *PFE '01: Revised Papers from the 4th International Workshop on Software Product-Family Engineering*, p. 13-21, Springer-Verlag, London, UK, 2002.

[BUD 03] BUDINSKY F., BRODSKY S.A., MERKS E., *Eclipse Modeling Framework (EMF)*, Pearson Education, 2003.

[CAC 06] *CACM, Software Product Line Engineering*, vol. 49, ACM Press, December 2006.

[CAL 03] CALDER M., KOLBERG M., MAGILL E.H., MARGANIEC S.R., "Feature interaction: a critical review and considered forecast", *Computer Networks*, vol. 41, no. 1, p. 115-141, 2003.

[CAR 90] CARRÉ B., GEIB J.-M., "The point of view notion for multiple inheritance", *OOPSLA / ECOOP*, p. 312-321, 1990.

[CAR 09] CARNEGIE MELLON UNIVERSITY, The Software Engineering Institute, last visited in June 2009.

[CHE 09] CHEN L., BABAR M.A., ALI N., "Variability management in software product lines: a systematic review", *Proceedings of the 13th Software Product Line International Conference*, San Francisco, CA, USA, August 2009.

[CLA 10] CLASSEN A., HEYMANS P., SCHOBBENS P.-Y., LEGAY A., RASKIN J.-F., "Model-checking lots of systems", *ICSE Proceedings, IEEE*, 2010.

[CLE 01] CLEMENTS P., NORTHROP L., NORTHROP L.M., *Software Product Lines: Practices and Patterns*, Addison-Wesley Professional, August 2001.

[CLE 02a] CLEMENTS P.C., "On the importance of product line scope", *PFE '01: Revised Papers from the 4th International Workshop on Software Product-Family Engineering*, p. 70-78, Springer-Verlag, London, UK, 2002.

[CLE 02b] CLEMENTS P., NORTHROP L., *Software Product Lines: Practices and Patterns*, Addison-Wesley, Boston, MA, USA, 2002.

[CLE 06] CLEMENTS P.C., JONES L.G., MCGREGOR J.D., NORTHROP L.M., "Getting there from here: a roadmap for software product line adoption", *Communications of the ACM*, vol. 49, no. 12, p. 33-36, December 2006.

[CZA 99] CZARNECKI K., EISENECKER U.W., "Components and generative programming", *Proceedings of ESEC-FSE 1999*, p. 2-19, 1999.

[CZA 00] CZARNECKI K., EISENECKER U.W., *Generative Programming: Methods, Tools, and Applications*, ACM Press/Addison-Wesley Publishing Company, New York, USA, 2000.

[CZA 02] CZARNECKI K., BEDNASCH T., UNGER P., EISENECKER U.W., "Generative programming for embedded software: an industrial experience report", *Proceedings of the 1st Conference on Generative Programming and Component Engineering*, p. 156-172, Springer-Verlag, 2002.

[CZA 03] CZARNECKI K., HELSEN S., "Classification of model transformation approaches", *OOPSLA '03 Workshop on Generative Techniques in the Context of Model-Driven Architecture*, October 2003.

[CZA 04] CZARNECKI K., HELSEN S., EISENECKER U.W., "Staged configuration using feature models", *Proceedings of the 3rd Software Product Line Conference 2004*, p. 266-282, Springer, LNCS 3154, 2004.

[CZA 05a] CZARNECKI K., ANTKIEWICZ M., "Mapping features to models: a template approach based on superimposed variants", GLÜCK R., LOWRY M.R. (eds), *GPCE, Lecture Notes in Computer Science*, vol. 3676, p. 422-437, Springer, 2005.

[CZA 05b] CZARNECKI K., HELSEN S., EISENECKER U.W., "Staged configuration through specialization and multilevel configuration of feature models", *Software Process: Improvement and Practice*, vol. 10, no. 2, p. 143-169, 2005.

[CZA 06a] CZARNECKI K., HELSEN S., "Feature-based survey of model transformation approaches", *IBM Systems Journal*, vol. 45, no. 3, p. 621-645, 2006.

[CZA 06b] CZARNECKI K., PIETROSZEK K., "Verifying feature-based model templates against well-formedness OCL constraints", JARZABEK S., SCHMIDT D.C., VELDHUIZEN T.L. (eds), *GPCE*, p. 211-220, ACM, 2006.

[DAS 05] DASHOFY E.M., VAN DER HOEK A., TAYLOR R.N., "A comprehensive approach for the development of modular software architecture description languages", *ACM Transactions on Software Engineering and Methodology*, vol. 14, no. 2, p. 199-245, 2005.

[DHU 08] DHUNGANA D., GRÜNBACHER P., RABISER R., "Decisionking: A flexible and extensible tool for integrated variability modeling", *Proceedings of the 2nd International Workshop on Variability Modelling of Software-intensive Systems*, Essen, Germany, January 2008.

[ECM 11] ECMDA, European Conference on Modelling Foundations and Applications, last visited in May 2011, http://www.utwente.nl/ewi/ecmfa/.

[EGE 09] EGEA M., RUSU V., "Formal executable semantics for conformance in the mde framework", *Innovations in Systems and Software Engineering*, vol. 6, p. 73-81, 2009.

[ELS 08] ELSNER C., FIEGE L., GROHER I., JÄGER M., SCHWANNINGER C., VÖLTER M., Ample project. deliverable d5.3 - implementation of first case study: Smart home, Technical report, December 2008.

[EME 04] EMERSON M., SZTIPANOVITS J., BAPTY T., "A MOF-based metamodeling environment", *Journal of Universal Computer Science*, vol. 10, p. 1357-1382, October 2004.

[FOR 08] FORSTER T., MUTHIG D., PECH D., "Understanding decision models, visualization and complexity reduction of software variability", *Proceedings of the 2nd International Workshop on Variability Modeling of Software-intensive Systems*, Essen, Germany, January 2008.

[FRA 01] FRANCE R., BIEMAN J., "Multi-view software evolution: a UML-based framework for evolving object-oriented software", *Software Maintenance, IEEE Computer Society*, p. 386-395, 2001.

[FRA 05] FRAKES W.B., KANG K., "Software reuse research: status and future", *IEEE Transactions on Software Engineering*, vol. 31, no. 7, p. 529-536, 2005.

[FRA 09] France Telecom, SmartQVT: An open source model transformation tool implementing the MOF 2.0 QVT-Operational language, Website, last visited in June 2009. http://smartqvt.elibel.tm.fr/.

[GAR 07] GARCES K., PARRA C., ARBOLEDA H., YIE A., CASALLAS R., "Variability management in a model-driven software product line", *Avances en Sistemas e Informática*, vol. 4, no. 2, p. 3-12, 2007.

[GOM 04] GOMAA H., *Designing Software Product Lines with UML: From Use Cases to Pattern-Based Software Architectures*, Addison Wesley Longman Publishing Co., Inc., Redwood City, CA, USA, 2004.

[GPC 11] GPCE, Conference on Generative Programming and Component Engineering, last visited in May 2011, http://program-transformation.org/GPCE11.

[GRO 08] GROHER I., SCHWANNINGER C., VÖLTER M., "An integrated aspect-oriented model-driven software product line tool suite", *ICSE Companion '08: Companion of the 30th International Conference on Software Engineering*, p. 939-940, ACM, New York, USA, 2008.

[HAL 08] HALLSTEINSEN S., HINCHEY M., PARK S., SCHMID K., "Dynamic software product lines", *IEEE Computer*, vol. 41, no. 4, p. 93-95, 2008.

[HOA 69] HOARE C.A.R., "An axiomatic basis for computer programming", *Communications of the ACM*, vol. 12, no. 10, p. 576-580, and p. 583, October 1969.

[JÉZ 08] JÉZÉQUEL J.-M., "Model driven design and aspect weaving", *Software and System Modeling*, vol. 7, no. 2, p. 209-218, 2008.

[JOU 05] JOUAULT F., KURTEV I., "Transforming models with ATL", *MoDELS Satellite Events, Lecture Notes in Computer Science*, vol. 3844, p. 128-138, Springer, 2005.

[JOU 06] JOUAULT F., KURTEV I., "On the architectural alignment of ATL and QVT", *SAC '06: Proceedings of the 2006 ACM Symposium on Applied Computing*, p. 1188-1195, ACM, New York, USA, 2006.

[KAN 90] KANG K., COHEN S., HESS J., NOWAK W., PETERSON S., Feature-oriented domain analysis (foda) feasibility study, Technical Report CMU/SEI-90-TR-21, 1990.

[KAN 98] KANG K.C., KIM S., LEE J., KIM K., SHIN E., HUH M., "Form: a feature-oriented reuse method with domain-specific reference architectures", *Annals of Software Engineering*, vol. 5, p. 143-168, 1998.

[KIC 97] KICZALES G., LAMPING J., MENDHEKAR A., MAEDA C., LOPES C., LOINGTIER J.-M., IRWIN J., "Aspect-oriented programming", AKSIT M., MATSUOKA S. (eds), *Proceedings ECOOP '97, LNCS*, vol. 1241, p. 220-242, Springer-Verlag, Jyvaskyla, Finland, June 1997.

[KRU 95] KRUCHTEN P., "The 4 + 1 view model of architecture", *IEEE Software*, vol. 12, no. 6, p. 42-50, 1995.

[KRU 06] KRUEGER C.W., "New methods in software product line practice", *Commununications of the ACM*, vol. 49, no. 12, p. 37-40, December 2006.

[KÜH 05] KÜHNE T., "What is a model?", *Language Engineering for Model-Driven Software Development, Dagstuhl Seminar Proceedings*, vol. 04101, 2005.

[LAW 07] Lawley M., Raymond K., "Implementing a practical declarative logic-based model transformation engine", *SAC '07: Proceedings of the 2007 ACM Symposium on Applied Computing*, p. 971-977, ACM, New York, USA, 2007.

[LIN 07] van der Linden F., Schmid K., Rommes E., *Software Product Lines in Actions: The Best Industrial Practices in Product Line Enginering*, Springer, 2007.

[LLO 94] Lloyd J.W., "Practical advantages of declarative programming", *Joint Conference on Declarative Programming*, 1994.

[LOU 08] Loughran N., Sanchez P., Garcia A., Fuentes L., "Language support for managing variability in architectural models", *Proceeding of the 7th International Symposium on Software Composition, Lecture Notes in Computer Science*, vol. 4954, p. 36-51, Springer, Budapest, Hungary, March 2008.

[LU 05] Lu S., Halang W.A., "Platform-independent specification of component architectures for embedded real-time systems based on an extended UML", Atkinson C., Bunse C., Gross H.G., Peper C. (eds), *Component-Based Software Development for Embedded Systems, Lecture Notes in Computer Science*, vol. 3778, p. 123-142, Springer-Verlag, Berlin Heidelberg, 2005.

[MAG 96] Magee J., Kramer J., "Dynamic structure in software architectures", *Proceedings of the 4th ACM SIGSOFT Symposium on the Foundations of Software Engineering, ACM Software Engineering Notes*, vol. 21, p. 3-14, ACM Press, New York, October 16-18 1996.

[MAG 10] No Magic, Inc. Magicdraw, http://www.magicdraw.com/, 2010.

[MAP 11] MAPLE, International Workshop on Model-driven Approaches in Software Product Line Engineering, last visited in May 2011, http://sites.lero.ie/maple2010.

[McG 03] McGregor J.D., The evolution of product line assets, Technical Report CMU/SEI-2003-TR-005, Software Engineering Institute, Carnegie Mellon University, June 2003.

[McI 68] McIlroy M., "Mass produced software components: software engineering concepts and techniques", *Proceedings of NATO Conference on Software Engineering*, p. 88-98, 1968.

[MDP 11] MDPLE, International Workshop on Model-Driven Product Line Engineering, last visited in May 2011, http://sites.lero.ie/mdple2010/.

[MED 00] MEDVIDOVIC N., TAYLOR R.N., "A classification and comparison framework for software architecture description languages" *IEEE Transactions on Software Engineering*, vol. 26, no. 1, p. 70-93, 2000.

[MER 05] MERNIK M., HEERING J., SLOANE A.M., "When and how to develop domain-specific languages", *ACM Computing Surveys*, vol. 37, no. 4, p. 316-344, 2005.

[MIT 08] MITSCHKE R., EICHBERG M., "Supporting the evolution of software product lines", *ECMDA Traceability Workshop (ECMDA-TW) 2008 Proceedings*, p. 87-96, 2008.

[MOD 11] MODELS, International Conference on Model Driven Engineering Languages and Systems, last visited in May 2011, http://www.modelsconference.org/.

[MOH 08] MOHAN K., XU P., RAMESH B., "Improving the change-management process", *Communications of the ACM*, vol. 51, no. 5, p. 59-64, 2008.

[MUL 05] MULLER P.A., FLEUREY F., JÉZÉQUEL J.M., "Weaving executability into object-oriented meta-languages", BRIAND L.C., WILLIAMS C. (eds), *Proceedings of the 8th International on Model Driven Engineering Languages and Systems, Lecture Notes in Computer Science*, vol. 3713, p. 264-278, Springer, Montego Bay, Jamaica, October 2005.

[NEI 89] NEIGHBORS J.M., "Draco: A method for reingineering reusable software systems", *Software Reusability, Concepts and Models, ACM Frontier*, vol. I, p. 295-319, Addison-Wesley, 1989.

[NOR 02] NORTHROP L.M., "SEI's software product line tenets", *IEEE Software*, vol. 19, no. 4, p. 32-40, 2002.

[OAW 09] OAW, The Openarchitectureware Framework, last visited in June 2009, http://www.openarchitectureware.org/.

[OMG 03] OMG, Object Management Group, Model driven architecture, mda guide version 1.0.1, Technical report, June 2003, http://www.omg.org/mda/.

[OMG 06a] OMG, Object Management Group, Meta object facility (MOF) 2.0. query/view/transformation specification, Technical report, http://www.omg.org/spec/QVT/, January 2006.

[OMG 06b] OMG, Object Management Group, Meta object facility, MOF specification version 2.0. Technical report, www.omg.org/, January 2006.

[OMM 00] VAN OMMERING R., VAN DER LINDEN F., JEFF K., MAGEE J., "The Koala component model for consumer electronics software", *Computer*, vol. 33, no. 3, p. 78-85, March 2000.

[OMM 02] VAN OMMERING R., "Building product populations with software components", *ICSE '02: Proceedings of the 24th International Conference on Software Engineering*, p. 255-265, ACM, New York, USA, 2002.

[OSG 09] OSGi Alliance, OSGI framework, last visited in June 2009. http://osgi.org/.

[PAN 07] PANTEL M., ACADIE team, OLC team, TOPCASED team, "The topcased project - a toolkit in open source for critical applications and systems design", *TOOLS EUROPE/Model-Driven Development Tool Implementers Forum (MDD-TIF)*, Zurich, Switzerland, 2007.

[PAR 76] PARNAS D.L., "On the design and development of program families", *IEEE Transactions on Software Engineering*, vol. 2, no. 1, p. 1-9, March 1976.

[PAR 09] PARRA C.A., BLANC X., DUCHIEN L., "Context awareness for dynamic service-oriented product lines", MUTHIG D., MCGREGOR J.D. (eds), *SPLC, ACM International Conference Proceeding Series*, vol. 446, p. 131-140, ACM, 2009.

[PAV 04] PAVEL S., NOYÉ J., ROYER J.-C., "Dynamic configuration of software product lines in archjava", NORD R.L. (ed.), *Software Product Lines: 3rd International Conference*, Lecture Notes in Computer Science, no. 3154, p. 90-109, Springer-Verlag, Boston, MA, USA, September 2004.

[PER 08] PERROUIN G., KLEIN J., GUELFI N., JÉZÉQUEL J.-M., "Reconciling automation and flexibility in product derivation", *SPLC*, p. 339-348, IEEE Computer Society, 2008.

[POH 05a] POHL K., BCKLE G., VAN DER LINDEN F., *Software Product Line Engineering – Foundations, Principles, and Techniques*, Springer, Heidelberg, 2005.

[POH 05b] POHL K., BÖCKLE G., VAN DER LINDEN F., *Software Product Line Engineering: Foundations, Principles, and Techniques*, Springer, Berlin, 2005.

[POH 06a] POHL K., METZGER A., "Software product line testing", *Communications of the ACM*, vol. 49, no. 12, p. 78-81, December 2006.

[POH 06b] POHL K., METZGER A., "Variability management in software product line engineering", *ICSE '06: Proceedings of the 28th International Conference on Software Engineering*, p. 1049-1050, ACM, New York, USA, 2006.

[PUR 10] Pure Systems, Pure::variants, 2010, http://www.pure-systems.com/pure_variants.49.0.html.

[RAS 11] RASHID A., ROYER J.-C., RUMMLER A. (eds), *Aspect-Oriented, Model-Driven Software Product Lines*, Cambridge University Press, United Kingdom, 2011.

[REI 09] 10th International Conference on Feature Interactions (icfi 2009), Lisbon, Portugal, June 2009. http://www27.cs.kobe-u.ac.jp/wiki/icfi/index.php.

[RIC 02] RICHTERS M., GOGOLLA M., "OCL: Syntax, semantics, and tools", CLARK T., WARMER J. (eds), *Object Modeling with the OCL, The Rationale behind the Object Constraint Language*, vol. 2263, *Lecture Notes in Computer Science*, p. 42-68, Springer, 2002.

[RIE 02] RIEBISCH M., BÖLLERT K., STREITFERDT D., PHILIPPOW I., "Extending feature diagrams with uml multiplicities", *Proceedings of the 6th World Conference on Integrated Design & Process Technology (IDPT2002)*, Pasadena, California, 2002.

[ROM 09a] ROMERO A., Derivación en lineas de productos de software dirigidas por modelos usando modelos de decision, PhD thesis, Universidad de Los Andes, Bogotá, Colombia, July 2009.

[ROM 09b] ROMERO A., ARBOLEDA H., "Modelos de decisión como mecanismo decomposición de reglas de transformación", *Paradigma*, vol. 3, no. 2, August 2009.

[RYD 79] RYDER B.G., "Constructing the call graph of a program", *IEEE Transactions on Software Engineering*, vol. 5, no. 3, p. 216-226, 1979.

[SAN 08] SANCHEZ P., LOUGHRAN N., FUENTES L., GARCIA A., "Engineering languages for specifying product-derivation processes in software-product lines", *Proceedings of the 1st International Conference in Software Language Engineering (SLE '08)*, Toulouse, France, September 2008.

[SHI 89] SHILLING J.J., SWEENEY P.F., "Three steps to views: extending the object-oriented paradigm", MEYROWITZ N. (ed.), *Proceedings of the 1989 ACM Conference on Object-Oriented Programming Systems, Languages and Applications*, p. 353-362, ACM SIGPLAN, New Orleans, Louisiana, October 1989.

[SIN 07] SINNEMA M., DEELSTRA S., "Classifying variability modeling techniques", *Information and Software Technology*, vol. 49, no. 7, p. 717-739, 2007.

[SMI 04] SMITH M.K., WELTY C., MCGUINNESS D.L., OWL web ontology language guide, world wide web consortium, Technical report, February W3C Recommendation 10 February 2004.

[SPL 11] SPLC, Software Product Line Conference, last visited in May 2011, http://www.splc.net/.

[STA 06] STAHL T., VÖLTER M., CZARNECKI K., *Model-Driven Software Development: Technology, Engineering, Management*, John Wiley & Sons, 2006.

[STA 73] STACHOWIAK H. (ed.), *Allgemeine Modelltheorie*, Springer, 1973.

[SUG 06] SUGUMARAN V., PARK S., KANG K.C., "Introduction", *Communications of the ACM*, vol. 49, no. 12, p. 28-32, 2006.

[SVA 05] SVAHNBERG M., VAN GURP J., BOSCH J., "A taxonomy of variability realization techniques", *Software Practice and Experience*, vol. 35, no. 8, p. 705-754, July 2005.

[TRA 06] TRASK B., ROMAN A., PANISCOTTI D., BHANOT V., "Using model-driven engineering to complement software product line engineering in developing software defined radio components and applications", *SPLC*, p. 192-202, IEEE Computer Society, 2006.

[VÖL 05] VÖLTER M., "Patterns for handling cross-cutting concerns in model-driven software development", *Proceedings of the 10th European Conference on Pattern Languages of Programs (EuroPLoP)*, Irsee, Bavaria, Germany, July 2005.

[VÖL 07a] VÖLTER M., GROHER I., "Handling variability in model transformations and generators", *Proceedings of the 7th Workshop on Domain-Specific Modeling (DSM '07) at OOPSLA '07*, 2007.

[VÖL 07b] VÖLTER M., GROHER I., "Product line implementation using aspect-oriented and model-driven software development", *Proceedings of the 11th International Software Product Line Conference*, p. 233-242, 2007.

[WAG 05] WAGELAAR D., "Context-driven model refinement", *MDAFA*, Lecture Notes in Computer Science, vol. 3599, p. 189-203, Springer, 2005.

[WAG 08a] WAGELAAR D., "Composition techniques for rule-based model transformation languages", *ICMT '08: Proceedings of the 1st International Conference on Theory and Practice of Model Transformations*, p. 152-167, Springer-Verlag, Berlin, Heidelberg, 2008.

[WAG 08b] WAGELAAR D., Platform ontologies for the model-driven architecture, PhD thesis, April 2008.

[ZIA 06] ZIADI T., JÉZÉQUEL J.-M., "Software product line engineering with the UML: deriving products", KÄKÖIÄ T., DUEÑAS J.C. (eds), *Software Product Lines*, p. 557-588, Springer, 2006.

Index